## AYN RAND WAS WRONG.
## ATLAS NEVER SHRUGGED!
# BITCOIN
#### A 50 YEAR OLD DREAM

**AYN RAND WAS WRONG.**
**ATLAS SHRUGGED!**
**BITCOIN**

Copyright© Saadettin Konukseven & Tuna Özen

**EDITOR:** Ece Berktav Çelik
**TRANSLATION:** Hasan Süpürgeci
**COVER DESIGN:** Sergen Temel Bayram
**ART DIRECTION:** Tuğba Özbek
2018 JULY

AYN RAND WAS WRONG.
ATLAS NEVER SHRUGGED!

# BITCOIN

A 50 YEAR OLD DREAM

Saadettin Konukseven & Tuna Özen

English Translation:
Hasan Süpürgeci

"In a few years teenagers in Indiana will be swapping over-the-blockchain derivatives with grandmas in India without asking New York City."

Nick Szabo

Dedicated to
Ayn Rand
Friedrich Hayek
Tim May
David Chaum
Ralph C. Merkle
Phil Zimmermann
Nick Szabo
Wei Dai
Hal Finney
and all the other geniuses that we have never heard of...
and all the beautiful people who have supported Bitcoin, or the idea of a currency that is not tied to any state, since day one...

# CONTENTS

| | |
|---|---|
| How Money Is Virtualized? | 17 |
| Evolution of Money | 25 |
| How Bitcoin Was Born? | 37 |
| Blockchain Technology | 67 |
| Smart Contracts | 91 |
| Areas of Use for Blockchain Technology | 97 |
| ICOs (Initial Coin Offerings) | 107 |
| Who is Satoshi Nakamoto? | 115 |
| Bitcoin Whitepaper | 129 |
| What Will Be The Value of Bitcoin? | 129 |
| Thanks | 153 |
| References | 155 |

# Bitcoin: Atlas Never Shrugged!

In Ayn Rand's Atlas Shrugged, all the people who work, contribute and produce start disappearing one by one as a result of the government attempting to take over all lines of work. These people are convinced to disappear by a man called John Galt. The whole country asks the same question, which also happens to be the motto for the book: "Who is John Galt?"

Due to Bitcoin becoming so well-known and having regular appearances on headlines, everyone started looking for the creator of Bitcoin, who is still a mystery. Just like Atlas Shrugged, a similar question gnawed at the minds of people and made headlines: "Who is Satoshi Nakamoto?"

Why did we start with such a prologue? Because you cannot understand Bitcoin without reading Ayn Rand and understanding Friedrich Hayek.

Because every revolution has an ideal foundation. Even though Bitcoin is a software revolution, it is also an ideal one. A revolution with roots reaching to the first days of humanity. A revolution that will take humans back to their essence. A revolution that may bring "Capitalism: The Unknown Ideal", as Ayn Rand calls it.

Bitcoin is a revolution against all third parties whom we believe to be trustworthy. It is a revolution against governments, banks, land registry offices, notaries and all intermediaries. It may very well be the foundation of a new world where only those who produce will rise, where borders will disappear; the utopia founded by John Galt for the hard-working people.

The media did not say that a revolution has happened when the French Revolution occurred in 1789. People didn't start thinking, "the concept of nation state is born and a new era has begun." Only after 100-150 years it was understood that this movement was a revolution that marked the end of an era and the beginning of a new one. Bitcoin is not understood at all right now. There aren't many that do understand it, save for the few people who invented it and paved the way for its invention. After 100 years, history books will say that the age of nation states that started with the French Revolution came to an end with the Bitcoin revolution.

**Ayn Rand was wrong. Atlas never shrugged!**

# What is Bitcoin?

The answers given to the question "What is Bitcoin?" resemble the elephant story told in Rumi's Masnavi.

"How do you describe an elephant in a dark room? Everyone will grab a different limb of the giant animal when you ask them to "describe the elephant." Someone will hold the ear, another the trunk and one will hold the foot. And each will define the elephant as something utterly distinct depending on which limb they have in their hand. Yet, the elephant is none of those. Maybe it is all of them, but no single part can define the elephant as a whole.

This is the case we have with Bitcoin. Software developers grab it from one place and provide a definition. Economists grab another limb and provide a different definition. Lawyers hold it from somewhere else and provide a completely different definition. Sociologists get a hold of it from another place and provide a definition like a sociologist would.

Long story short, everyone has their own, unique definition of Bitcoin. Bitcoin is all and none of these definitions.

- Without looking at the origins of money,
- Without understanding what money is,
- Without comprehending human instincts (or common sense) which have been a part of us since day one,
- Without realizing that the existing monetary system has nothing to do with the system you believe to exist,
- Without understanding the philosophy, beliefs and purposes of the inventors of Bitcoin and those who pioneered this revolution,

- Without understanding why laws exist,
- Without realizing that the third parties we trust in bilateral transactions are nothing but sand castles,

You cannot understand Bitcoin. Maybe you can, but not completely. If you do not question your current perceptions now, 5 years from now, you will be asking yourself "where did I fail?"

That's why, it's "time to turn on the lights."

Enjoy.

## What is Not Included in This Book?

You will not find financial advice in this book.

You will not find predictions about Bitcoin's price in this book.

You will not find advices for becoming rich overnight in this book.

You will not find a complicated narration that will confuse you with cool buzzwords in this book.

You will not find the answers to all the questions in your mind...

On the contrary, more question marks will pop in your head after reading this book. You will question more.

# CHAPTER ONE

## HOW IS MONEY VIRTUALIZED?

CHAPTER ONE

# How is money virtualized?

Most probably, you have heard of Bitcoin as the "virtual currency", like many people did. Because everything that is produced on the computer, that is not tangible, that exists on and transferred over the Internet can be defined as "virtual."

The media, too, has slapped this very label on Bitcoin without looking much into what it is. Even though it's been 9 years since the invention of Bitcoin, the media still continue to define it as the virtual currency. After all, the dollar is physical as it is printed in a printing house and can be held in hand. Or is it not?

Let's assume that you have a physical $10 bill. You go to the bank and deposit it. Your $10 is in your bank account. Mr. Smith comes over and asks for a $10 loan from your bank. And you bank hands the $10 bill to Mr. Smith. Let's go back to the day Mr. Smith took the loan and check the financial table:

- You have $10. (Rather, you think that you have $10 in your bank account.)

You

Mr. Smith

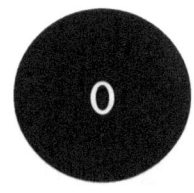
Bank

- Mr. Smith has a physical $10 bill.
- The bank has no money.

Just think about millions of similar transactions happening over and over again. This is how the current financial system works in a nutshell. We used the most basic financial product, namely loans, as an example. Now, think about hundreds of derivatives like loans being created. This is how money becomes virtualized. This is how financial crises are created.

The 2008 global crisis erupted with the "mortgage" loan, one of the dozens of financial instruments available. Let's adapt our example to this crisis.

Mr. Smith receives a $10 loan from the bank to buy a house. Mr. Smith takes that $10 and buys a house with the money. For the first year, everything works out fine; Mr. Smith can pay his loan with ease. The system is running like a clockwork. At the end of the first year, Mr. Smith owes the bank $9. Suddenly, Mr. Smith becomes unemployed. 3 months pass by and Mr. Smith still cannot find a job as the economy is getting worse.

Left without a job, Mr. Smith starts skipping on his loan payments. So the bank takes Mr. Smith's house from him. But only $6 is offered to the same house, even though it was worth $10 last year. The bank sells the house regardless and has $6.

You need money and you go to the bank to withdraw some. Guess what? You thought you had $10 in the bank but the bank has only $6. The bank cannot pay you.

You

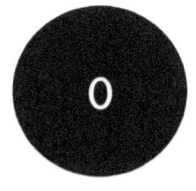
Mr. Smith

Bank

This is exactly what the 2008 crisis was. This incident, which we have stripped down to its essence, has happened to millions of people with hundreds of thousands of dollars in each case. And turned into a global crisis that affected us all.

So, how do we come up with a solution to the aforementioned problem? Yes, just like you thought: By printing money. By printing more money in every bottleneck, in every hiccup of the system.

One of the smartest suggestions after the 2008 crisis came from former soccer player Eric Cantona:

"We don't pick up weapons to kill people to start the revolution. The revolution is really easy to do these days. What's the system? The system is built on the power of the banks. So it must be destroyed through the banks. We must go to the bank. In this case there would be a real revolution. It's not complicated; instead of going on the streets and driving kilometres by car you simply go to the bank in your country and withdraw your money, and if there are

a lot of people withdrawing their money the system collapses. No weapons, no blood, or anything like that."

Cantona was not taken seriously, on account that he was just an athlete. Moreover, his suggestion was discredited by the media. Cantona said what none of the economy professors who appeared on the media and who had big titles before their names said. And yes, Cantona was right.

The money that we believed to be in our bank accounts were never there to begin with. They were just a string of virtual numbers. The $10 we deposited into the bank has turned into $1000 with hundreds of derivatives. So, $990 was created virtually.

At this point you may say that the banks need to keep a "required reserve." You would be right. But this rule is applicable to banks in developing countries. However, in 2008, we have also seen that this rule is not applicable to the banks with highest credit scores in developed countries.

Think about the financial institutions that lead the 2008 crisis. The largest financial institutions of the world came to the brink of bankruptcy, not the smaller ones in developing countries. Then they did go bankrupt. But the governments were rescued with the money paid by ordinary taxpayers. Because the system was completely dependent on these leviathans. These institutions going bust meant that the whole system would collapse.

So how did these gigantic financial institutions arrived on the verge of bankruptcy despite numerous rules and measures? Because their credibility was almost never questioned. They had A++++ credit scores. They were the cornerstones of the system. And that was the problem. The existing financial system is built on unquestioned belief, trust and fear. We just believe in the financial institutions that we presume to be colossal. We think that they are safe and they cannot be "hacked."

When Satoshi Nakamoto was creating Bitcoin,
- he was proposing an alternative to the existing financial system
- that could not be sustained anymore, and to all transactions occurring between two parties that required a trusted 3rd party:

"Let's stop trusting a 3rd party we deem to be trustworthy in transactions occurring between two people. Instead, let's look at the encrypted proofs in the blockchain technology."

To put it simply, Satoshi Nakamoto was proposing a rational mindset instead of an unquestioned trust in humans.

# CHAPTER TWO

## EVOLUTION OF MONEY

"Give me control of a nation's money and I care not who makes its laws."

Mayer Amschel Rotschild

CHAPTER TWO
------

## What is money?

Contrary to popular belief, we start trading not when we use money, but when we are still in the womb. While receiving the nutrients and minerals required for our survival from our mother, we offer joy and excitement to her in return. Long story short, we make a virtual payment in exchange for tangible gains. This might sound cruel and cold. Nevertheless, it is the truth.

Even though the term trading is disliked, or even frowned upon, the single thing that enables us to survive is our ability to trade. Because as humans we, unfortunately, need one another. Trading is what enabled humankind to reach today.

Consider this, can you survive or lead a better life on your own? Let's say you have sown some wheat, baked your bread, cooked your veggies, built your house, took water from the well.. Can you generate your own electricity? Can you perform surgery on yourself? To put it briefly, you need good neighbors. Trading has allowed humanity to progress and survive. Let's take it one step further and say "trading is what enabled the human race to survive as a species." From this point of view, trading is the greatest human invention.

Bartering was the method for trading in the early days of humanity. Bartering allowed people to survive at that time and was sufficient for trading. You could give 1 kg of wheat to cover your need for 2 kg of apples, for instance. But as time passed, bartering became insufficient for humanity's needs. Because it was hard to calculate the exact cross-values of each product. Also, the person with the apples may have needed milk, not wheat. This caused a lack of overlapping between supply and demand. At this point, a common trading tool which meant something for all humans was needed.

According to Nick Szabo, who is one of the few people who can lay the foundation of the concept of money and the historical evolution of money, each transaction has a "mental cost." This mental cost is very high in barter economy. Because, you have to know the price of each product against all others for trading to function properly in this economy. For example, you have to know the price of you apples in wheat, barley, coal, etc. This increased the mental cost and made trading harder for humans. We can safely say that the underlying reason for coming up with a common currency was to reduce said mental cost, thereby facilitating trade. Of course, humanity could not achieve a single universal currency. So apples had prices in various currencies in different countries. Yet, the "mental cost" was quite lower compared to bartering. The two most widespread currencies used by mankind, until bills, were as follows.

1.  Substances containing calcium carbonate which are biologically available in crystallized form such as pearls and seashells.

2.  Precious metals such as gold and silver.[2]

When we think about why humans chose these two types of substances as a tool for trading, we come across the following results.

- They are transferable to coming generations via inheritance due to their durability
- They are limited in terms of supply
- They are the bounty of nature

Basically, humanity has always tried to protect itself against inflation and to have a free trading tool since day one. Even though

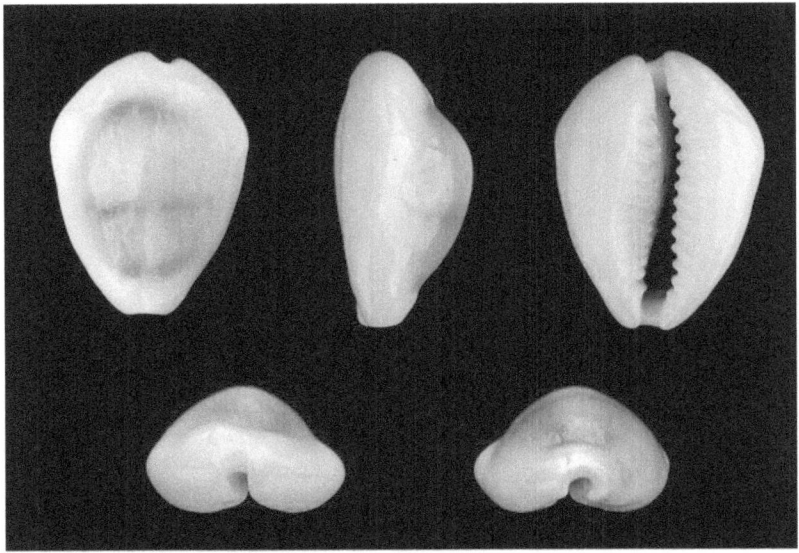

the mankind's accumulated knowledge was low at the beginning, survival instinct has allowed them to find the right way somehow. We, as modern day people, consider ourselves to be smarter than prehistoric humans. But frankly, that's not quite the case.

According to widespread belief, you think that the money printed by governments has a reserve, don't you? You think that countries cannot print money whenever they want to, that they cannot devalue you money.

Following World War II, countries have signed the "International Monetary Agreement" in the town of Bretton Woods in US, in order to facilitate international trading. A fixed exchange rate was determined for the currencies of all participating countries and it was agreed that the value of said currencies will be settled according to the US dollar. According to this agreement, only the US dollar was pegged to gold and the United States agreed to give 35 ounces of gold to each country that brought 1000 US dollars.

People still think that the printing of money depends on the gold in their treasury, on the assumption that the agreement still stands. Because the common was informed of the agreement. They heard it from their teachers, from their mothers and from the media. But the fact that the agreement is over and that the US can print as much mney as it likes have not been covered so much.

In 1971, the United States has declared that it opted out of the "Bretton Woods

Agreement." This date marks the beginning of an era where money can be printed without being pegged to anything. We can also say that it marks the beginning of an era where money lost its freedom, its independence and was put into shackles.

## Evolution of Money

Looking at the evolution of money, we see that humans have used "tangible, limited bounties of nature" as money so far. However, in modern times, money is just an abstract idea. Money is a belief that humans have agreed upon. Think about the dollar. We all agree on the value of a dollar. But the dollar is merely a piece of paper. It bears no value except for the cost of printing. And it has no equivalent reserve.

Maybe you have all of these before. Maybe you haven't. Or, maybe, it didn't sound that convincing.

Let's take a look at the evolution of the dollar.

Here's what is written on this $50 from 1778:

"This bill entitles the bearer to receive Fifty Spanish milled dollars, or the value thereof in Gold or Silver, according to a Resolution passed by CONGRESS at Philadelphia, September 26th, 1778."

*50 dollars dated 1778 / U.S. Diplomacy Center exhibition page*

Basically this bill says: This thing that you are holding is not a worthless piece of paper. The treasury has its reserve in gold or silver.

*National Numismatic Collection, National Museum of American History.*

The coin which is shown above in both sides is a Gold One Dollar from 1849. The smallest dollar unit made of gold. It seems like a local Philadelphia newspaper, Public Ledger, noticed the problems to be caused in the long run by not supporting the Gold Dollar. Here is what they said in an article from December, 1936: "The dollar is the smallest gold coin that would be convenient, and as it would be eminently so, neither silver nor paper should be allowed to take its place."[3] To give an example as to how this coin resisted inflation; we can say that as of 2017, this Gold One Dollar is worth $110 when melted.

If you noticed, this $1 bill from 1928 says "United States Note." That is to say, it's been printed by the US Treasury. Also, it is mentioned that equivalent value is present in the US Treasury.

$1 bill with Silver Certificate from 1928. This bill from the US Treasury is deposited in silver in the treasury. It says "One Silver Dollar" on the bottom part of the bill.

*National Numismatic Collection, National Museum of American History.*

These Silver Certified $1 bills remained in circulation from 1928 to 1957. Until 1968, people who had these bills were able to receive silver from the treasury by submitting these bills. After 1968, however, only dollar bills with "Federal Reserve Note" written on top were handed from the treasury in return for this money. Considering that the Bretton Woods Agreement ended in 1971, we can assume that the unrequited silver dollars signaled the impending death of the agreement.

*National Numismatic Collection, National Museum of American History.*

## Let's Talk About Today

Looking at the money we have mentioned and shown, it is obvious that these were not just pieces of paper and the country's treasury had the reserve in gold or silver to back them.

This is what the common man thinks about money anyway. We believe that the bills in our pockets are backed by gold or silver, that dollars cannot be printed without any physical basis.

On the next page, you can see two $1 bills. There is not printing mistake or negligence. Both are $1 bills, right? Yes, at first glance, they are both $1 bills. They look almost identical. But the reality is, there is a huge difference between them. There is a gigantic finan-

*National Numismatic Collection, National Museum of American History.*

cial system difference between them. There is difference between them that is the reason for all the wars on the globe.

Take a look again; the one on the above says "United States Note." It's backed by the US Treasury. It's reserved in the US Treasury. The one below says "Federal Reserve Note" on top. Which means that it is a bill printed by FED, a private bank. A bill that is not that related to the US Treasury.

And that is the evidence for the virtualization of money in the last century. That is the evidence of humanity's transition from limited, physical bounties of nature to a mere piece of paper, to virtual money.

Maybe it is the veil of mystery over former US President John F. Kennedy's assassination who wanted to stop the dollar from being a "Federal Reserve Note" and hand it back to the Treasury to bring back the "United States Note"...

## *In God We Trust*

Another interesting point is that the "In God We Trust" expression was not present on the dollar until 1953. This expression was first added to the dollars printed by the US Treasury in 1953. The bills printed by the Treasury did not have their reserves in "gold or

*Barry Goldberg Archieve, barrygoldberg.net*

silver" at this given date. They were bills that were printed solely on the basis of trust. The expression was added to the dollar bills printed by FED from 1965 onwards. This may very well be the biggest change we can observe in money... Transition from a tangible monetary system to a trust-based system...

# CHAPTER THREE

## HOW WAS BITCOIN BORN?

"The difference between bad and well-developed digital cash will determine whether we have a dictatorship or a real democracy."

David Chaum

CHAPTER THREE

## How was Bitcoin born?

Labeled as "virtual money" or "money without any government backing" by the existing financial system, Bitcoin was born as a solution for the virtualization of money in the last century, for the loss of guarantee behind money and for the bloated financial system that can no longer be sustained.

Like all inventions, Bitcoin did not appear out of the blue overnight. It developed as a result of efforts that lasted for years, ideas that were refined and finally appeared with an article published in 2009 by a person or people with the pseudonym of Satoshi Nakamoto.

The dream of a banking system and a currency that are not connected to any government was realized with Bitcoin. But the foundation of this dream goes way back. There were always people who were festered with the destruction of gold standard.

It's not "Technology advanced and Bitcoin was born." We can say that "the idea of a free currency that is not tied to any government was always there and finally technology allowed it to be created."

Nick Szabo, one of the pioneers of Bitcoin's underlying blockchain technology and the creator of the "smart contract" concept, started a presentation on the blockchain technology by thanking Ayn Rand, Tim May and Friedrich Hayek.

We cannot understand the ideal foundation of Bitcoin without understanding these people and those who have worked hard in the stages leading up to the creation of Bitcoin.

Photo: Ayn Rand Institute

## Ayn Rand

While all -ism's (ideologies) were morally defended, there weren't many that were eager to do so for capitalism. Those who advocated capitalism always did that by putting the economic benefits in the forefront. That's still the case. As a matter of fact, there aren't many who defend capitalism out loud. Ayn Rand, on the other hand, was defending capitalism from a moral point of view. She claimed that true freedom could only be achieved by the liberation of individuals and that capitalism was the only system that could do it. While almost all thinkers and societies considered money to be the root of all evil, Ayn Rand believed that money was the source of things good. According to Rand, paper money was the root of all evil. Dubbing her philosophy "Objectivism," Ayn Rand claimed that all objective criteria died and the efforts of mankind were left in the hands of papers without any future or value when the gold standard was renounced.

"Whenever destroyers appear among men, they start by destroying money, for money is men's protection and the base of a moral existence. Destroyers seize gold and leave to its owners a counterfeit pile of paper. This kills all objective standards and delivers men into the arbitrary power of an arbitrary setter of values. Gold was an objective value, an equivalent of wealth produced. Paper is a mortgage on wealth that does not exist, backed by a gun aimed at those who are expected to produce it. Paper is a check drawn by legal looters upon an account which is not theirs: upon the virtue of the victims. Watch for the day when it becomes, marked: 'Account overdrawn.'"

(Ayn Rand, Atlas Shrugged)

## Friedrich Hayek

A Nobel winning economist, he was probably the most contrarian among economists in history. It may be baffling for someone who hasn't read anything from Friedrich Hayek that there are hundreds of cryptocurrencies.

If Friedrich Hayek were to rise from the dead and see a website where cryptocurrencies were traded, he would most probably tear up. Hayek proposed the privatization of money in his book titled The Denationalization of Money. He was terrified of the idea that the state had a monopoly over money while everything was privatized.

Hayek was against all sorts of centralization and central planning. He believed that free market was not only the source for a better economy, but also the enabler of individual liberties. Thinking that the economy is shaped by the independent behaviors of people who are not aware of one another, Hayek claimed that a free market could not be artificially created but would only occur on its own. He said that the ups and downs of economy were normal and the intervention of the government in the economy only made things worse.

Now it is easier to understand why those proposing a financial system without a center against all centralized systems thank Hayek. Don't you think Hayek is describing Bitcoin in his words from 1984?

"I don't believe we shall ever have a good money again before we take the thing out of the hands of government. We can't take it violently out of the hands of government, all can do is by some sly roundabout way introduce something they cannot stop."

## Tim May and the Cypherpunk Movement

When you start looking into the roots of Bitcoin and the people who have contributed to its development, the first thing that you will see will be the "Cypherpunk Movement" that started in the end of 80s. Cypherpunk is derived from the word "Cypher" and "punk."

Tim May, one of the founders of the Cypherpunk Movement,

claimed that anarcho-capitalism could be realized at least in the cyber-realm.

According to May, the advent of the Internet and encryption technologies allow two people to communicate, conduct businesses and even sign digital contracts with total anonymity. He ended his "Crypto-Anarchist Manifest", where he voiced his opinions in 1988, with the following sentence:

"We have nothing to lose but our chains."

## David Chaum

David Chaum realized the electronic currency system he proposed in 1983, "e-cash", via his company DigiCash in 1990. You were able to convert your money from the bank to e-cash and download it to your computer. Then you could use this money while shopping at places that accepted e-cash. Even though it was so ahead of its time, DigiCash went bankrupt in 1998. Compared to the costs of using credit cards in those years, e-cash had both lower costs and provided anonymity to the user as if they were using cash.

DigiCash had also signed agreements with banks such as Credit Suisse and Deutsche Bank. But the reason why these banks accepted DigiCash was to avoid being left behind, not to be pioneers. Banks made good money from credit cards and the consumers were not concerned about privacy. Maybe it wasn't the right time for an electronic monetary system.[4]

David Chaum's employees believed that his personality played a major role in the bankruptcy of DigiCash. He refused buying orders from Microsoft and Visa by raising the price too high.

Having a bit of a paranoid stature, maybe Chaum was right in his own way. In an interview from 1996, he said:

"The difference between bad and well-developed digital cash will determine whether we have a dictatorship or a real democracy."

The biggest difference between "e-cash" and Bitcoin, and the electronic money transfer systems which can be considered as the

*Steven Levy's article about e-cash published in Wired*

progenitors of Bitcoin, was that it did not supply its own currency. "E-cash" was not a currency, it was just an untraceable electronic money transfer system.

The fact that Nick Szabo worked at DigiCash for about a year is just one of the examples showing that those who chased the idea of Bitcoin are just a handful of people.

## DMT (Digital Monetary Trust)

The Internet-based and untraceable banking project DMT was the brain child of J. Orlin Grabbe. You were able to keep and/or transfer currencies and precious metals such as gold, dollar, yen in your anonymous account.

DMT also came up with their own currency called "DMT Rand." It was named after Ayn Rand, the most ardent defender of capitalism.

## b-money

Moved by the "Crypto-Anarchist Manifest" of Tim May, Wei Dai believed that an anonymous and untraceable trading tool, namely a brand new currency and money transfer was required for a truly free and anonymous society to exist in the cyber realm.

What Wei Dai suggested in this regard was "b-money" in 1998. B-money remained only on paper and was never realized. Wei Dai proposed two alternative protocols for b-money in his article. What set b-money apart from Bitcoin was that the supply of money was unlimited.

In the Q&A section of his website, Wei Dai states that he still doesn't think that the limited supply of Bitcoin makes much sense. Responding to a question about the future of Bitcoin in 2014 by saying that he was not interested in cryptocurrencies since 1998, Wei Dai can be labeled as a genius beyond his time.

Dai is also the second person to be contacted by Satoshi Nakamoto for referencing b-money before publishing his article on Bitcoin.

## BitGold

The closest proposal to Bitcoin came from Nick Szabo in 1998. According to Szabo, precious metals were far more valuable and safe compared to the currencies provided by states. But there were two problems pertaining to precious metals. First, it was nearly impossible to use precious metals in smaller transactions. Second, it was costly and problematic to handle precious metals from one place to another due to issues such as safety and accidents.

BitGold was the system proposed by Szabo in this regard. Produced inside computers, BitGolds were supposed to provide a great advantage in terms of production and transfer costs. Furthermore, they could be used in daily transactions as they could be divided into units as small as desired. The main difference between BitGold and Bitcoin was that supply had no limit. With BitGold, money was going to be created in direct proportion to the energy consumed. The "mining" concept used in Bitcoin was first utilized in BitGold.

6-7 months before Satoshi Nakamoto published his Bitcoin article, Nick Szabo wrote in his blog that the shortages in BitGold were covered and he wanted to start it up. However, right after the Bitcoin article was published, Szabo removed the blog article and republished later after changing the publication date. This increased the number of claims stating that Szabo is Satoshi Nakamoto.

Even though Satoshi Nakamoto does not refer to Szabo's Bit-Gold in his Bitcoin article, he said that Bitcoin was the realized version of "b-money" and "BitGold" in the Bitcoin forum.

## RPOW (Reusable Proofs of Work)

### Reusable Proofs of Work
Hal Finney

Inspired by Nick Szabo's "Collectibles" theory, Hal Finney developed RPOW. RPOW is based on the "Proof of Work" protocol, just like Bitcoin. From this perspective, RPOW may be considered as the first prototype of Bitcoin.

While Nick Szabo's BitGold and Wei Dai's b-money remained only as articles, RPOW may be called the only system that was turned into a software before Bitcoin. Contrary to Bitcoin, RPOW does have a trusted 3rd party (intermediary). A transparent "server" checks to see whether a double spending occurs and confirms the transaction when sending a "coin" from one person to another. Acting as the trusted 3rd party, this "server" differs from the conventional "trusted 3rd parties" in that it has a transparent structure.

But RPOW was not created for coming up with a monetary form.

## Bitcoin: (A peer to peer electronic cash system)

As you can see, DigiCash, DMT and other untraceable electronic money transfer systems that we did not mention here were not successful. When Satoshi Nakamoto published the first version of Bitcoin, it was mentioned that there was an initiative called "Open Coin" in the UK, to which he replied:

 ⁊⁊ Reply by Satoshi Nakamoto on February 15, 2009 at 16:42
Could be. They're talking about the old Chaumian central mint stuff, but maybe only because that was the only thing available. Maybe they would be interested in going in a new direction.

A lot of people automatically dismiss e-currency as a lost cause because of all the companies that failed since the 1990's. I hope it's obvious it was only the centrally controlled nature of those systems that doomed them. I think this is the first time we're trying a decentralized, non-trust-based system.

"A lot of people automtically dismiss e-currency as a lost beacuse of all the companies that failed since the 1990's. I hope it's obvious it was only the centrally controlled nature of those systems that doomed them. I think this is the first time we're trying a decentralized, non-trust-based system."

It is apparent that there were many ideas that were similar to Bitcoin. All the technologies used in Bitcoin were already invented. But it was necessary to come up with a completely new idea using the existing ones. Maybe it's not a coincidence that Bitcoin came to life in 2009. The 2008 crisis must have affected someone or some people who are preoccupied with this subject.

## Bitcoin P2P e-cash paper  *2008-11-01 19:16:33 UTC*

I've been working on a new electronic cash system that's fully peer-to-peer, with no trusted third party.

The paper is available at:
http://www.bitcoin.org/bitcoin.pdf

The main properties:
Double-spending is prevented with a peer-to-peer network.
No mint or other trusted parties.
Participants can be anonymous.
New coins are made from Hashcash style proof-of-work.
The proof-of-work for new coin generation also powers the network to prevent double-spending.

Bitcoin: A Peer-to-Peer Electronic Cash System

Abstract. A purely peer-to-peer version of electronic cash would allow online payments to be sent directly from one party to another without the burdens of going through a financial institution. Digital signatures provide part of the solution, but the main benefits are lost if a trusted party is still required to prevent double-spending. We propose a solution to the double-spending problem using a peer-to-peer network. The network timestamps transactions by hashing them into an ongoing chain of hash-based proof-of-work, forming a record that cannot be changed without redoing the proof-of-work. The longest chain not only serves as proof of the sequence of events witnessed, but proof that it came from the largest pool of CPU power. As long as honest nodes control the most CPU power on the network, they can generate the longest chain and outpace any attackers. The network itself requires minimal structure. Messages are broadcasted on a best effort basis, and nodes can leave and rejoin the network at will, accepting the longest proof-of-work chain as proof of what happened while they were gone.

Full paper at:
http://www.bitcoin.org/bitcoin.pdf

Satoshi Nakamoto

---------------------------------------------------------------------

The Cryptography Mailing List
Unsubscribe by sending "unsubscribe cryptography" to [EMAIL PROTECTED]

*First e-mail containing the Bitcoin article shared by*
*Satoshi Nakamoto in the Cryptography Mail Group*

For, you can see the headline of The Times dated Jan 3, 2009 in the code contained in the Genesis block of Bitcoin:

*"Times 3 Ocak 2009. The Times 03/Jan 2009. Chancellor on brink of second bailout for banks."*

The content of the news article tells that the state considers the options of re-injecting the huge sums of money obtained from taxes back into the economy or taking on the toxic assets of banks. (Toxic assets are the assets that have almost no financial value.)

## Can a currency that is not tied to any state, central bank and banking system succeed?

This is probably a question you asked yourself when you first heard of Bitcoin and most likely you couldn't find an answer.

After all, everyone took the easy way and called Bitcoin a "virtual currency" when describing it.

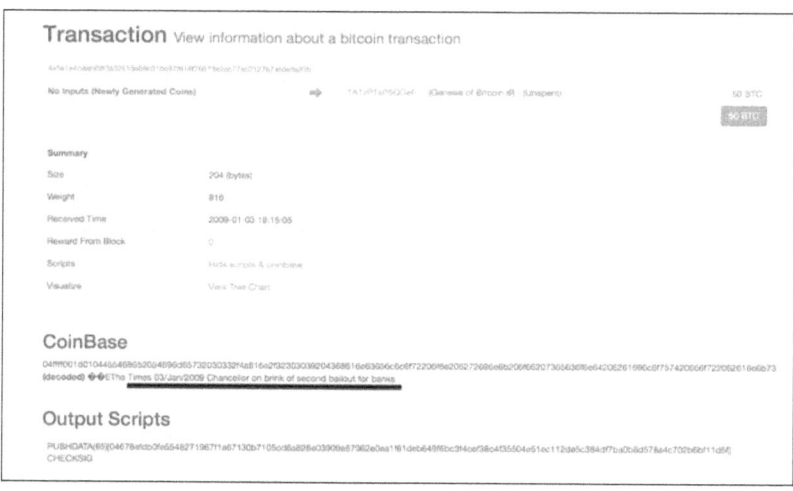

*Genesis Block of Bitcoin and the message contained therein*

## HOW WAS BITCOIN BORN?

*Headline from The Times, January 3, 2009
which is included in the code of the Bitcoin Genesis Block*

Most probably you thought, "Everything is digitalized, now it's money's turn." Yet the dollars in bank accounts have already been digitalized. What's the point of having this new thing? "If such a thing exists, it will only be a bubble," you said. And you are completely right. Such as currency is a bubble at best. It cannot even be a bubble. There have been certain attempts that did not even make it to bubble-hood. And all of them failed.

## How do existing currency systems run and what is required for a currency to be successful?

There are two essential elements for a currency to succeed and survive. These are the shackles put on currencies.

1.) A central bank that will determine the monetary policies for the currency.

2.) A banking system that enables the currency to be transferred among bank accounts.

For instance, the dollar is dependent on FED. FED decides the fate of the American monetary policy, and thus, the dollar. And dollars are transferred across the globe via Swift. The reason why the dollar is a strong and widespread currency is that it takes its power from FED, US and Swift.

But the dollar is also a really weak currency. Because it is shackled by the FED, US and Swift.

# HOW WAS BITCOIN BORN?

## Bitcoin v0.1 released  2009-01-09 20:05:49 UTC

Announcing the first release of Bitcoin, a new electronic cash system that uses a peer-to-peer network to prevent double-spending. It's completely decentralized with no server or central authority.

See bitcoin.org for screenshots.

Download link:
http://downloads.sourceforge.net/bitcoin/bitcoin-0.1.0.rar

Windows only for now. Open source C++ code is included.

- Unpack the files into a directory
- Run BITCOIN.EXE
- It automatically connects to other nodes

If you can keep a node running that accepts incoming connections, you'll really be helping the network a lot. Port 8333 on your firewall needs to be open to receive incoming connections.

The software is still alpha and experimental. There's no guarantee the system's state won't have to be restarted at some point if it becomes necessary, although I've done everything I can to build in extensibility and versioning.

You can get coins by getting someone to send you some, or turn on Options->Generate Coins to run a node and generate blocks. I made the proof-of-work difficulty ridiculously easy to start with, so for a little while in the beginning a typical PC will be able to generate coins in just a few hours. It'll get a lot harder when competition makes the automatic adjustment drive up the difficulty. Generated coins must wait 120 blocks to mature before they can be spent.

There are two ways to send money. If the recipient is online, you can enter their IP address and it will connect, get a new public key and send the transaction with comments. If the recipient is not online, it is possible to send to their Bitcoin address, which is a hash of their public key that they give you. They'll receive the transaction the next time they connect and get the block it's in. This method has the disadvantage that no comment information is sent, and a bit of privacy may be lost if the address is used multiple times, but it is a useful alternative if both users can't be online at the same time or the recipient can't receive incoming connections.

Total circulation will be 21,000,000 coins. It'll be distributed to network nodes when they make blocks, with the amount cut in half every 4 years.

first 4 years: 10,500,000 coins
next 4 years: 5,250,000 coins
next 4 years: 2,625,000 coins
next 4 years: 1,312,500 coins
etc...

When that runs out, the system can support transaction fees if needed. It's based on open market competition, and there will probably always be nodes willing to process transactions for free.

Satoshi Nakamoto

--------------------------------------------------------------------
The Cryptography Mailing List
Unsubscribe by sending "unsubscribe cryptography" to
majord...@metzdowd.com

*Mail announcing that the 1st version of Bitcoin software is ready, shared by Satoshi Nakamoto in the Cryptography Mail Group*

## What is Bitcoin?

Bitcoin is not a virtual currency. Bitcoin is not just a currency either.

There is not central bank behind Bitcoin that determines the policies. Bitcoin is an alternative to all central banks. Bitcoin is a central bank whose rules have been laid out at the very beginning.

Bitcoin has no place in the existing money transfer system. Bitcoin is an alternative to the existing banking system. Bitcoin is an electronic money transfer system that enables value (Bitcoin) to be transferred between two people.

And Bitcoin is a currency. It is the currency of a central bank whose monetary policy has been determined in advance by the law of nature, mathematics. Bitcoin is the currency of an electronic money transfer system that does not require a trusted 3rd party. Bitcoin is not shackled. Bitcoin is a currency without shackles.

Bitcoin had to fulfill the abovementioned conditions in order to survive from 2009 to our day. Said conditions formed the intersection of the dreams of various people over the course of years. It is the answer to the questions no one could completely figure out until 2009.

In addition to these, people needed to attribute a value to Bitcoin. As we have said in previous pages; ultimately, money is a belief that people agree upon. That's why the rise of Bitcoin after the 2008 crisis made a group of people, however small, see Bitcoin as an alternative to the existing system.

## Why Bitcoin?

No invention is invented for no reason. Every invention solves a problem. Or rather, each invention solves dozens of problems and opens up new horizons by creating a domino effect.

So why did dozens of scientists dreamed of a currency that was not tied to any government, a money transfer system which could not be stopped by any force?

## Trustworthiness

First of all, we certainly require a trusted 3rd party while transferring money between two people. For instance, there is always an

## Centralized System
### Trusted 3rd Party

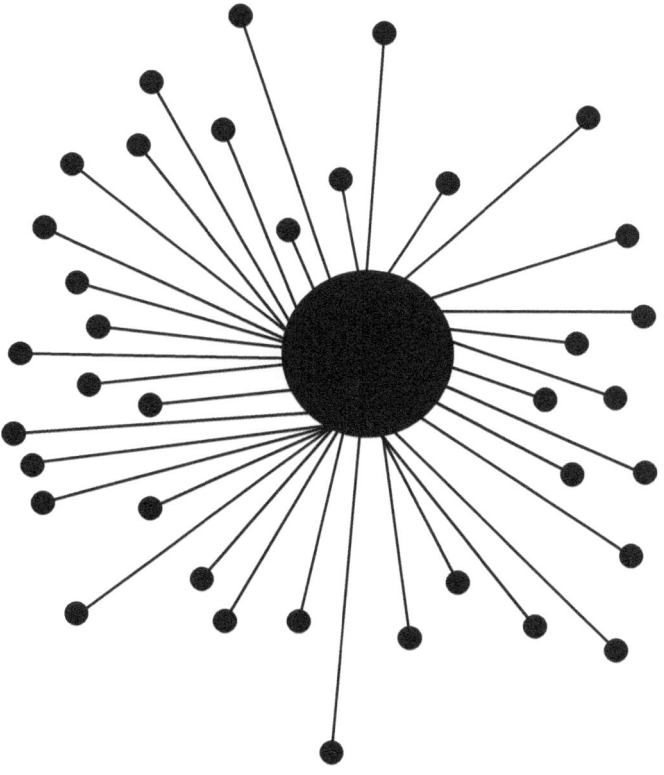

All data is stored at the trusted 3rd party

## Distributed Sytem

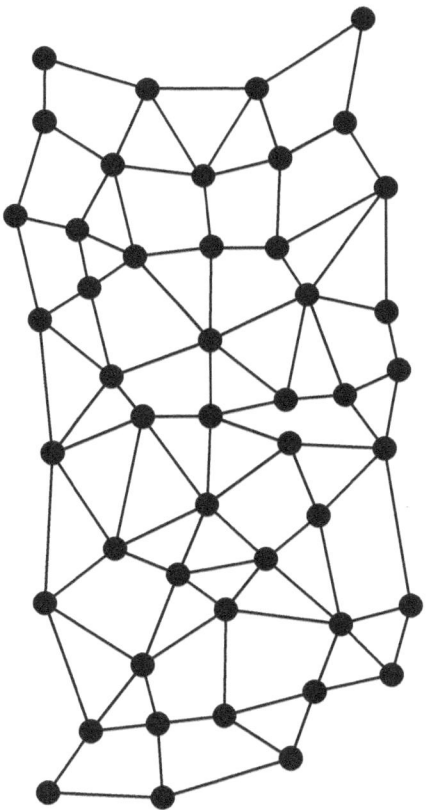

All data is stored at all the computers/servers connected to the network

intermediary bank when John is sending money to Smith. And in all these transactions, we always assume that this bank or intermediary institution is trustworthy. We ignore the possibility that this institution can be hacked, can go bankrupt or commit fraud.

Remember the İmar Bank incident in Turkey. The bank committed a really simple fraud. They were keeping double ledgers. The amounts shown to the customers and the amounts shown to the government were different. Thousands of people were wronged. Again, JP Morgan, which is presumed to be safe by millions of people, was hacked in 2015.

## Cost

Can a Zimbabwean refugee in Sweeden send $10 to his family in Zimbabwe? Of course he can. Only by paying a transaction fee that is almost higher than the amount he is sending. Despite all the progress in technology, sending money across the world is still very costly. As long as the banks preserve their monopoly and alternative money transfer systems are not found, it doesn't seem likely

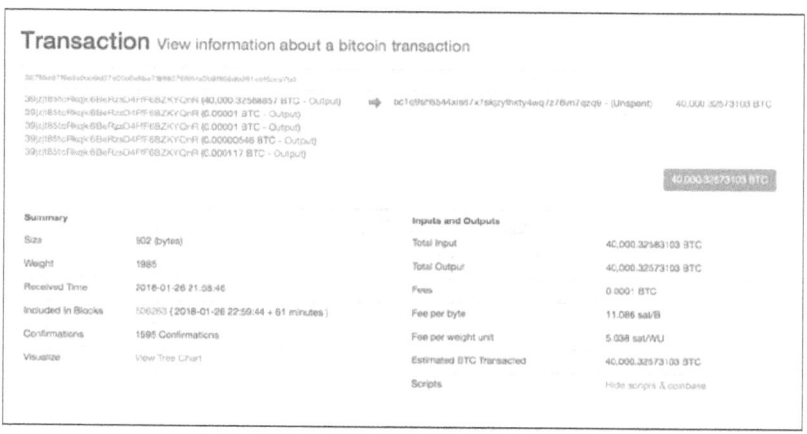

*A Bitcoin transfer over the Lightning Network in January 26, 2018.*
*40.000 Bitcoins were sent from one adress to another with only $1 transaction fee.*

that these fees will be lower. On top of that, there are millions of people without access to banking services.

As of 2018, Bitcoin is just a 9 year old technology. Even though Bitcoin transfer prices increase from time to time as demand for Bitcoin also increases; recently developed technologies such as Lightning and Segwit, and the technologies that are yet to be developed will enable Bitcoin transfers to be performed with lower fees.

You have probably heard of the news pieces published to create the perception that the energy consumed for mining Bitcoin is very high. Well, do you hear anyone talking about the cost of FED printing new dollars? Is there anyone talking about the energy consumed by the current money transfer systems that are running globally? The charts shown below and in the following page were taken from FED's website.

For example, the total cost of printing, handling, packaging 250 billion dollars worth of bills injected into circulation and the destruction of the damaged ones in 2016 was 1.1 billion dollars. This is

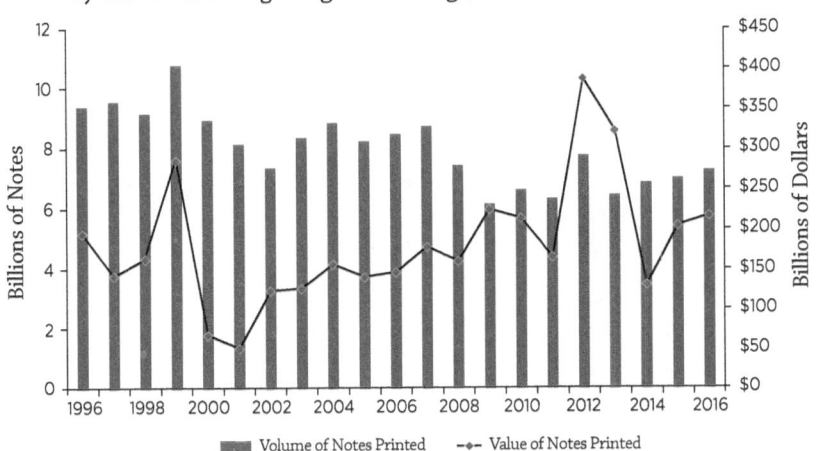

**Calendar-Year Print Order**
The volume and value of notes printed each year
by the Bureau of Engraving and Printing (Billions of notes and dollars)

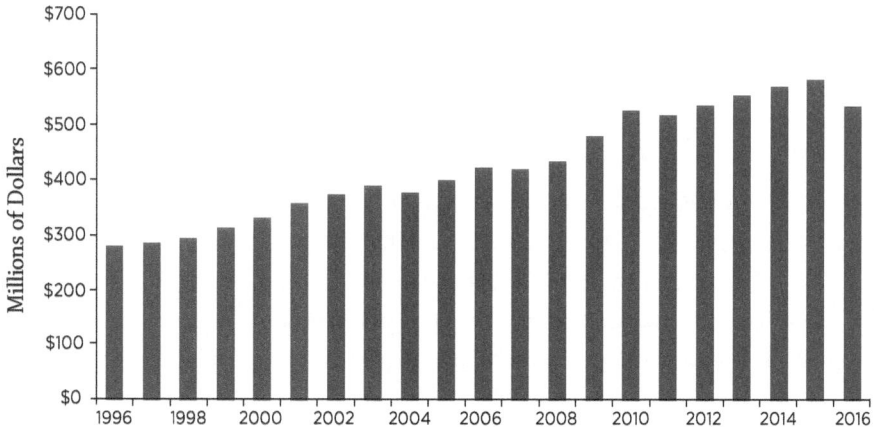

**Federal Reserve Expenses for Cash Operations**
Expenses include processing, receiving, verification, destruction, transportation, and non-standard packaging of currency

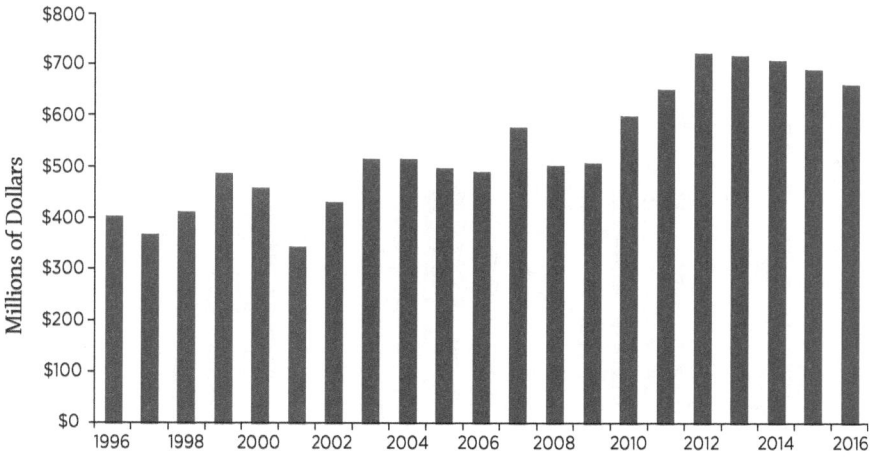

**Cost of New Currency**
Costs include printing, transportation, and destruction of mutilated currency

just the money spent for releasing said bills. We're not even talking about FED's operation expenses, data servers, security expenses and the salaries of the employees.

Let's leave FED's expenses and energy consumption aside. Because printing and releasing the money is not where it all ends. Think about the headquarters of banks and their thousands of branches. Think abou the servers and data centers allocated for banking transactions. Think about the electricity consumed, Internet data used for banking and the hordes of employees.

## Privacy

In the current financial system, personal privacy is almost non-existent. Since we have a trusted 3rd party in every bilateral money transfer, our identities, the amount of money we have in our account and the amount we sent to anyone is stored in the servers of these intermediary institutions. Bitcoin, on the other hand, is providing a completely different privacy model compared to the conventional system.

With Bitcoin, the names and identities of people are not used. But all Bitcoin transactions over the Bitcoin network are publicly available. Anyone who feels like it may examine all the transactions beginning from the first Bitcoin block. What they will see is only

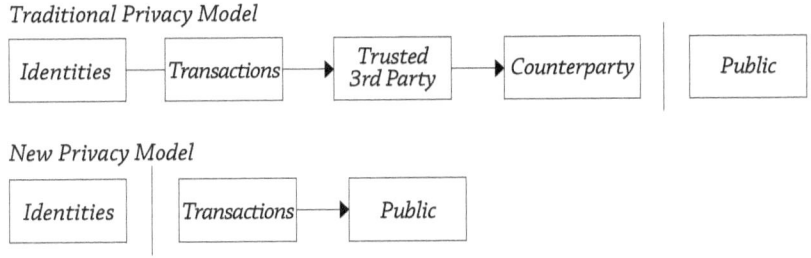

the Bitcoin addresses. For this reason, Bitcoin can be named both the most transparent and the most private money transfer system in the world.

You may ask, "why does Bitcoin follow such a method?" Satoshi Nakamoto proposed this solution, instead of the trusted 3rd party in the existing money transfer system, so that the "miners" included in the system can see all the past transactions to prevent "double spending."

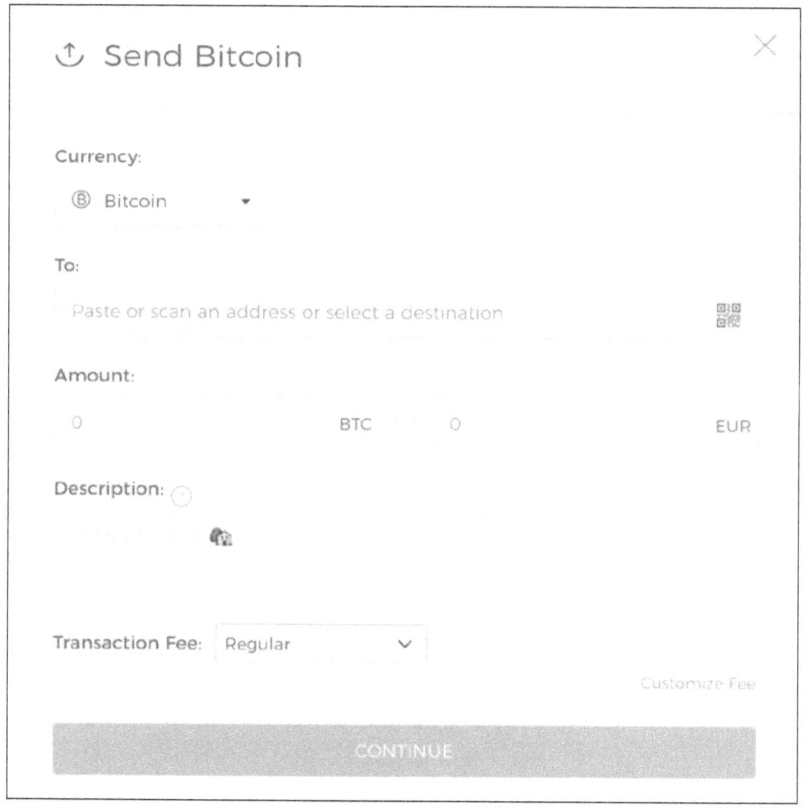

*Example of a Bitcoin wallet from blockchaininfo.com*

## Freedom

We all know the perennial embargo on Iran. Powerful states can lay embargoes on relatively weaker states under the pretext of a crime or at least "suspicion of a possible crime." And since they can monitor all the money flow in the international financial system, they can impose these sanctions quite easily.

So, the article which proposed a solution to all the aforementioned problems and which turned and old dream into reality was published in 2009 by a person or a group of people under the pseudonym of Satoshi Nakamoto.

With his Bitcoin article, Satoshi Nakamoto came up with a brand new alternative to the current financial system.

As proof of a transaction, Satoshi Nakamoto proposed the encrypted blockchain technology instead of a trusted 3rd party while transferring money between two people.

Thanks to the blockchain technology invented by Nakamoto,

1. The data related to the transaction between two people was to be stored in all computers/processors included in the network, not a single, central place. Computers/systems called "miners", which provided the processing power, ensured the safety of the network and the operation of the money transfer. The fact that those who provide the processing power required for network safety and system operation are called "miners" may show that Bitcoin was created to be a physical reserve currency for humanity, just like gold, silver and seashells were.

2. Low fees would be taken from bilateral money transfers. For instance, you pay a significantly smaller fee when sending money to a bank account in the same country, as opposed to sending money to a foreign account. Blockchain technology eliminates the concepts of national and international transfers.

3. Identities are not seen during the money transfer between two people. Only the Bitcoin addresses consisting of numbers and letters are seen.

Like all inventions, Bitcoin was founded by those who were against the system. Bitcoin's fate will come to an end when it becomes the system itself.

---

*How was the initial value of Bitcoin determined?*
*Let's assume that you invented Bitcoin. How would you determine the initial price? Bitcoin's initial value was calculated with a completely solid method. The cost of electricity required to generate one Bitcoin was the initial value. So, $1 = 1.309.*

# HOW WAS BITCOIN BORN?

# CHAPTER FOUR

## BLOCKCHAIN TECHNOLOGY

"Trusted third parties are security holes."
Nick Szabo

CHAPTER FOUR

## Blockchain technology

Let's say you took part in an election and cast your vote. How do you know that your vote has actually been counted?

You went to get a cup of coffee and seen information about the coffee you are about to purchase has been a part of a fair trade system. How do you know that you coffee was actually traded fairly?

Trust.

As we were taught to trust unconditionally and skip the ques-

tioning; we always have the same answer in our minds with such topics. "It's not possible, would such a big company do that??", "I'm sure they are keeping a close eye on these things, they cannot risk it."

This approach does not imply that any company or system is pursuing methods that are different than those presented to the public. We just want to stress that we ignore many similar processes in our daily lives by saying or thinking "it's not possible."

Most people consider Bitcoin as a virtual currency. If they knew about the rationale behind it, they would realize that it is something that we are actually familiar with, that it is a safer, traceable and fast system that can change countless standard procedures in our daily lives thanks to the opportunities presented by advancing technologies.

Actually, Bitcoin is just one of the applications running on a software system called "blockchain", which is technology's gift to us. Considering the possibilities offered by the blockchain technology, Bitcoin is just the tip of the iceberg. The opportunities it presents are only limited by your imagination.

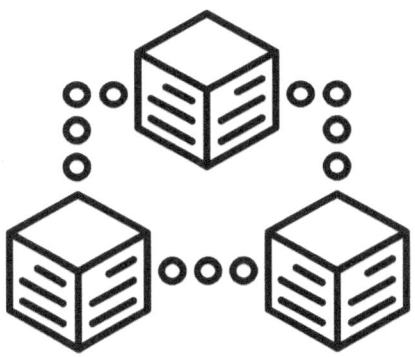

## So how does this blockchain system work?

Simply put, money exists to facilitate trading. The trading system has gradually grown and became increasingly complicated throughout the centuries. Everyone became able to trade with anyone on a global scale. In order to keep the relevant information safe, these transactions were first recorded in ledgers, then in computers. As time progressed and technology advanced, the methods we use for keeping these transactions have changed, but the mostly non-public and isolated manner of managing the information remained the same. That's why we always needed an intermediary person/institution to verify or have others verify/approve said information so far. States, banks, accountants, notaries etc. have assumed the role of the intermediary up until now. These intermediaries have always been called the "trusted third parties" on the assumption that they are indeed trustworthy. This is where the blockchain comes into play: to remove the trusted third parties from the equation.

Basically, the blockchain technology is the product of three separate systems operating in tandem. Cryptography for identity management, a network running among computers to record the data and the blockchain protocol which is the platform on which the transactions are performed.

The blockchain system, on which Bitcoin runs as well, enables a computer network which has all of its components connected to the Internet and which can record and keep all of the performed transfers and transactions, to store the whole process in the computers distributed across said network. Also, joining the network is completely free of charge and the system is open to anyone who wants partake in the process with their computers. The execution of the process in this manner prevents the transactions from being in a closed circuit or from being managed by a single person/institution. Instead, the information is recorded on and accessible from a single digital ledger which distributed throughout the whole network. This is the infrastructure utilized by Bitcoin, which you see on the news and read articles about on the Internet. Bitcoin is not really a "virtual currency"; it is simply an application that runs on the basis of the blockchain software and is supported by cryptography due to its working principles. Hopefully, you will rethink what the term "virtual money" actually means by the end of this book.

## Why is it called "blockchain"?

Data (information) is processed by the owners of computers connected to the network into blocks which have a certain data volume. When the data volume of a block is filled, new information is stored in the next block. Thus the blocks form a "blockchain."

These blocks record all transactions performed over the network through a single blockchain.

Basically, the information stored in the blocks are as follows:

- Time of transaction (date and time),
- Parties of transaction (Each user has two keys of their own. One is private, the other is public. When used together, these two keys which are created specifically for each user turn into a private, unique digital signature. Digital signatures of both parties serve as the parties of transaction inside the block.)
- Amount of transaction
- Hash (can be considered as a fingerprint and is specific to a certain block). It's the identity of the previous block. Therefore, if any change or arrangement regarding the Hash is desired to be monitored, this is quite easy. (The information collected during the transfer may vary depending on the blockchain.) The fact that a block contains a copy of the previous block's identity and its own identity forms the basis of the "chain" definition. There is only one block in this system which does not contain the identity of the previous. This is called the "Genesis Block." It's the first block in the chain and the whole chain is lined up after it.

Any computer included in the system contains a full and up-to-date copy of all information stored in the blockchain. Following calculations based on highly complex mathematical principles, all transactions performed in the blockchain are verified by the "miners." Basically, "miners" are the providers of the digital ledgers used for keeping transaction records. Same mathematical principles ensure that the miners are continuously agreeing upon all

> "Money at its core is simply a ledger for keeping track of debts and Bitcoin is truly the best iteration of a universal ledger we've ever seen."
> John Reed, Former Chairman & Ceo of Citibank

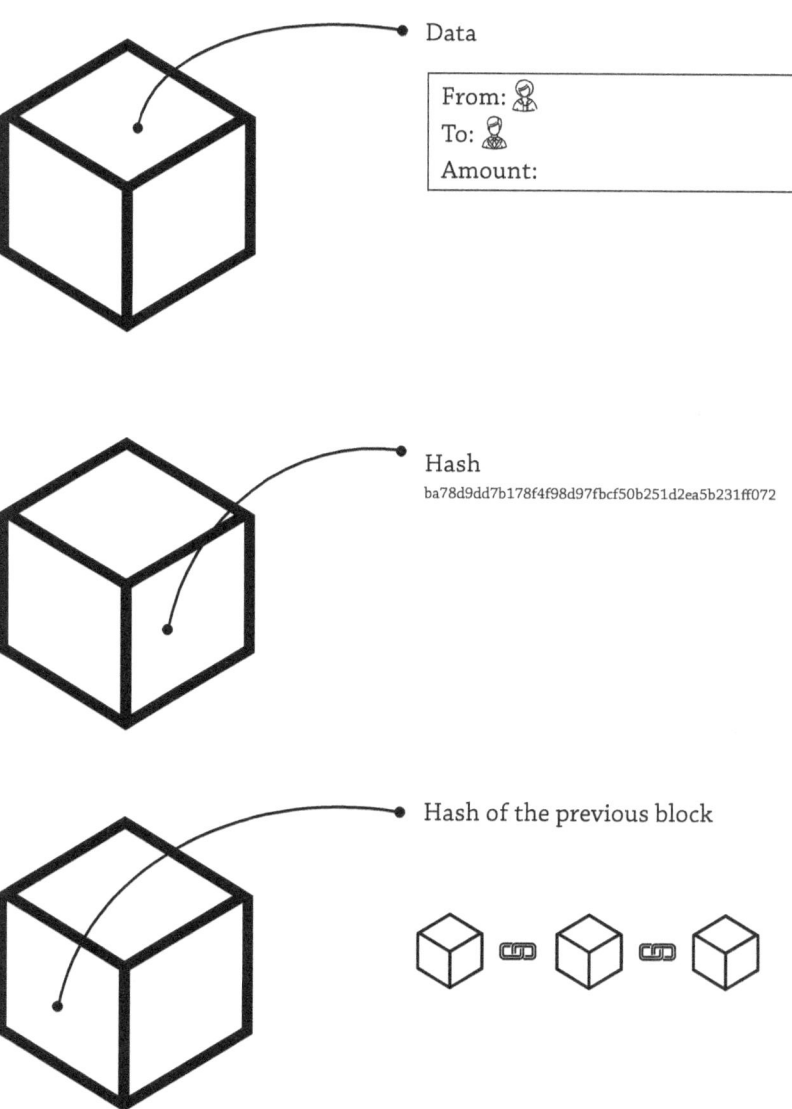

# BLOCKCHAIN TECHNOLOGY

## Centralised

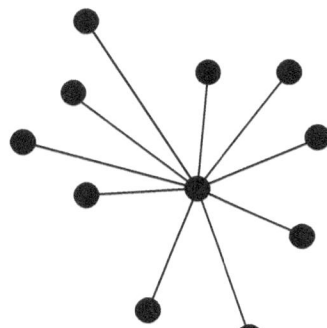

## Decentralised

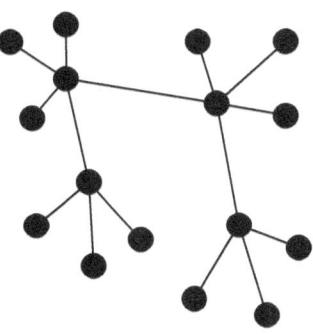

## Distributed Ledgers

Distributed ledgers can be public or private and vary in their structure and size
Public blockchains require computer processing power to confirm transactions (mining)

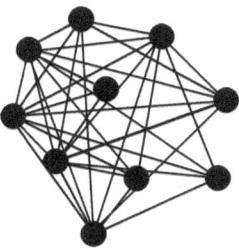

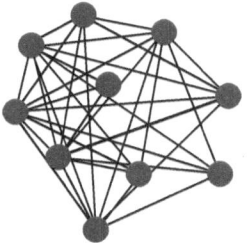

● Users are anonymous. Each user has a copy of the ledger and participates in confirming transactions independently.

● Users are not anonymous. Permission is required for users to have a copy of the ledger and participate in confirming transactions.

*Source: Blockgeeks, blockgeeks.com*

transactions happening in the chain. If there is any attempt at directing/manipulating a transaction in a way that would trick or hurt the system, the control mechanism of "persistent consensus within the network" prevents such misleading transactions from happening. Theoretically, you can think of it as a case where a single transaction is being anonymously audited by hundreds, even thousands of notaries. That's why blockchain is innately secure. Enabling safe transfer of money between individuals is only one of the numerous opportunities provided by this software system. It wouldn't be absurd to think about the opportunities it can bring in the near future.

## What actually happens when a new block is created?

After stringing to the end of the previous blockchain, the system has to reach a consensus on various topics in order to progress and include the next block into the chain. Such as "What is the condition of the existing chain?" "Is everything alright?", "What are the current statuses of the accounts in our electronic ledgers?"

How can the system act as one when the community of machines in the network do not trust each other? This is why consensus is needed. Consensus in the blockchain enables the system to more forward, work and decide as a single unit despite being a distributed mechanism.

## What does this system offer that is different than our conventional system?

• In the blockchain system, all values that you own are under your control. There is no third party that can approve or prevent transactions when you are accessing and transferring said values or when your authority over said value is restricted. You have total control.

When you visited your bank to withdraw a certain sum that you own, you may have heard the tellers say "You need to give us prior notice before you can withdraw such a sum of cash, your money will be ready tomorrow." The money is yours, you need it at that moment and you cannot access it; but why?
• The value you want to transfer can be transferred within few minutes and the transaction would be deemed as safe within a few hours, not days or weeks. Nowadays, you cannot even imagine having a money transfer via the conventional system (especially international transfers) approved within minutes.
• As anyone can verify each transaction on the blockchain at any times, full transparency exists. It is quite different than our current understanding of transparency, isn't it?
• Transfer fees are so low that they enable international micro-payments. We are not used to incidents of "cake be-

ing worth the candle", especially when it comes to money transfer. Yet, blockchain gives us this opportunity.
• Blockchain technology can also be utilized to create decentralized applications which can manage information and value transfer in a fast and secure way. This only limited by your imagination. The hot topic is mostly money and the transfer thereof, however, the blockchain technology can be used by developing various applications in many processes that are parts of our daily lives.

As is the case with each technological innovation, blockchain technology comes with its own challenges.
• The technology is still being improved and its still in the early stages of its development. As applications on a broader spectrum are created, improving the safety of the system becomes a necessity.
• Even though many trading platforms have appeared, it is not really easy or common to trade these tools and services. However, it's becoming increasingly widespread as it rapidly gains popularity. Furthermore, it is actually against the nature of the system that the trading platforms act as "trusted 3rd parties." But these phases should be covered for a decentralized future.
• While the anonymity of accounts provide a spectacular level of personal privacy for the users despite the traceability of the transactions, it also enables ill-intentioned, illegal money transfers as well. This is an outcome that makes it harder for legal institutions to track illegal activities. Nevertheless, we have to accept that each technology makes our lives easier and takes humanity further will have certain side effects.

While pleading during his trial, Phil Zimmermann, the inventor of PGP (an encrypted electronic mail system), illustrates this situation in a very nice way: "Like every new technology, this comes at some cost. Cars pollute the air and cause traffic jams."[5]

Naturally, privacy leads they way in the criticism against Bitcoin. In the end, who would want the drug trade and financing of terror to become easy in the world? But while this smear campaign is being run, the people's lack of "questioning" is being used again. Bitcoin was invented in 2009. Weren't drugs being sold in the world before 2009? Or, how much of the global drug trade is done via Bitcoin? Weren't terror funds transferred via the existing banking system before? Isn't the dollar still being used in these illegal activities?

## Mining

In traditional monetary systems, governments print money when they need or when required by their monetary policies. But in the Bitcoin cryptocurrency system money is not printed, it is discovered. This discovery is not an unlimited production without any rules, as is the case with money printed in print houses. The system awards those who enable the Bitcoin network to be secure and to run, by giving them the discovered Bitcoins.

## So what is the role of mining?

As we've covered in previous chapters, "miners" are people and units who are responsible for ensuring the transfers are realized, recorded and stored on the blockchain. People and unit stands for the computers connected to the blockchain. This can be any computer.

## A miner's adventure on the blockchain

*Let's say that Person A wants to send X amount of Bitcoin to Person B (this may be another crypto value as well). We see it as an instantaneous or fast transfer, depending on the infrastructure of the value being sent, from Person A's wallet to Person B's wallet; but how does the process really work?*

When the transfer request arrives, the miner performs the checks to see if the transaction can be realized or not:
-Does the transaction fulfill the required standards to be realized?
-Does the sender have at least the specified amount of resource (Bitcoin)?
-Are the sender and receiver addresses valid?
-When does this transfer happen? and so on...
Then, the miner unit continues working as follows:
"I have to collect all the information pertaining to this transfer and put it inside a block. I did that, what's next? What is the last block at the end of the chain while I work to realize this transaction? Let's say its block 513578. OK, then the new block I'm working on must contain this information as well.

Up until now; I have checked whether the transaction is valid, I received all necessary information and the hash of the block added to the end *of the chain right before the transaction I am about to perform. (Block 513578's hash)*

*Now?*

*Is everything prepared for adding the new block to the chain and for recording it on other computers where the chain is stored? Is the transaction over? No, there is one more step:*

*'I have to solve the Proof of Work problem."*

## What exactly is the problem that needs to be solved?

To put it simply, it is a complicated puzzle that requires processing power. Solving the puzzle is a hard and time-consuming process. Generally speaking, it can be considered as a safety and deterrence system. Finding the solution to the puzzle will take quite a while and the miner cannot have the block recorded on the chain without doing so. Therefore, the next block transaction cannot start and the miner will not be awarded. The miner may find the solution to the puzzle with a certain algorithm but may never know if it's correct or not without trying. That's why it uses all possible options of an algorithm to look for the solution of the puzzle until it reaches said solution. High processing power becomes important at this point. The more processing power the miner has, the more probably solutions it can try in a shorter time. The faster it solves the puzzle, the faster it reaches the next block reward. (That's why people are investing so much in computer hardware. That's why you friends are buying dozens of graphic cards or processors. Or the rigs manufactured solely for mining... It's all about solving the problem as quick as possible with as much processing power as you can afford.)

## Why is the Proof of Work system necessary?

Let's assume that you want to alter the content of a block insi-

 Someone requests a transaction.

The requested transaction is broadcast to a P2P network consisting of computers, known as nodes.

Validation:
The networks of nodes validates the transaction and the users status using known algorithms.

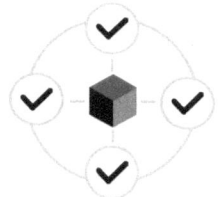 A verified transaction can involve cryptocurrency, contracts, records, or other information.

Once verified, the transaction is combined with other transactions to create a new block of data for the ledger.

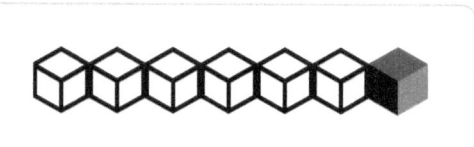

The new block is then added to the existing blockchain, in a way that is permanent and unalterable.

 The transaction is complete.

*Kaynak: Blockgeeks, blockgeeks.com*

de the chain. This automatically means that the fingerprint of the block, namely the hash, has to change. By the nature of blockchain, the last link in the chain must contain the fingerprint of the previous block. Automatically, this new information change has to be re-calculated and updated in all the blocks in the blockchain so that the existing chain remains valid.

The computers of our day are so powerful that they can re-calculate and store the changes resulting from this information alteration in seconds. That's where the "Proof of Work" comes into play. However, blockchain is utilizing the "Proof of Work" mechanism in order to slow down the process and prevent possible manipulation.

If we draw an example from the Bitcoin system, the process of creating a new block goes at a slower pace and a stable manner thanks to the Proof of Work mechanism. With Bitcoin, this mecha-

nism sets the calculation for each block and the addition of a new block to the chain in a slice of time that is close to 10 minutes. Therefore, if you plan on altering a block, this means that you have to go through the same process for each block behind the one that you are altering. This is a workload that is hard to overcome, regardless of how powerful your computer is. Let's assume that the number of processed blocks in the Bitcoin blockchain is 500,000 as of December 12, 2017,. In order for the slightest change in the 2nd block to be valid again, a re-calculation that will last more than 8 and a half years is required. It is worth reminding that the whole process is monitored by thousands of computers. That's why the gains obtained from hacking the system will be less than the cost of hacking. This is where the intrinsic safety of blockchain lies.

## Did Bitcoin come up with the Proof of Work?

The most well-known proof of work function is SHA-256. This just one of the many functions. You can think of this function as a member of the SHA-2 type algorithm family.

This measure was first used to limit e-mail and service denial attacks in 1997, under the name of "Hashcash." Invented by Adam Back, the ideal foundations of "Hashcash" were laid down in 1992-1993. Cynthia Dwork and Moni Naor are known as the pioneers of this field. So the Proof of Work system, like many concepts we believed to be discovered in conjunction with Bitcoin, have already been discovered way before. In addition to the numerous alternative PoW models, "Proof of Stake" is another widely used model. In all kinds of sources, you almost always see these concepts with their abbreviations, "PoW" and "PoS" respectively. The single difference between POS and POW is that the former utilizes a different verification method in the validation process. Instead of solving the puzzle to reach the reward, the verification system selects the verifier for the next block reward with a model which is random. However, the larger the investment in your wallet is, the higher your chances are for being selected in this "random" selection. (The more voting power you have in the executive board, the more probable it is to have the decision you desire.)

## The relation between Bitcoin and blockchain

The blockchain system, on which Bitcoin runs as well, does not actually care about what the value of Bitcoin represents. The value of a Bitcoin as a currency and what it represents are, in fact, determined by the blockchain users. One Bitcoin consists of one hundred million equal pieces. Each of these pieces can be programmed and defined separately. This enables the users to program each Bitcoin piece as, including but not limited to, a currency, a company share, energy in kilowatts per hour or a digital certificate. This function is one of the greatest indicators that Bitcoin stands for more than just currencies or payments.

## Wallets

Fundamentally, crypto value wallets exist for three reasons.
1. Seeing the current crypto value balance
2. Buying and sending crypto values
3. Storing and keeping crypto values

To reinforce with an easy example, wallets are not that different from the interfaces and applications you use for sending/receiving e-mails in principle. Just as we need such interfaces to send or receive our e-mails, we need crypto value wallets for basically the same reason.

One of the defining points of a wallet is where your private key is stored. So, let's elaborate on the "private key" topic which we have covered briefly under the Blockchain chapter.

## Private Key

You can think of the private key as a long string comprising numbers and letters. This combination string forms the key to your wallet.

Theoretically speaking, knowing the private key to a wallet would allow you to access the contents of that wallet (if no additional measures are taken).

Wallets and private keys are among the most essential parts where cryptography is involved in the system.

## WALLET TYPES

### Full Node Wallets

You can use these wallets on the desktop of your computer via a simple interface. Its main characteristic is that it keeps an up-to-date copy of the whole chain related to the crypto value you are using it for. You should be aware that the blockchain information will be stored in your computer, occupying some hard drive space.

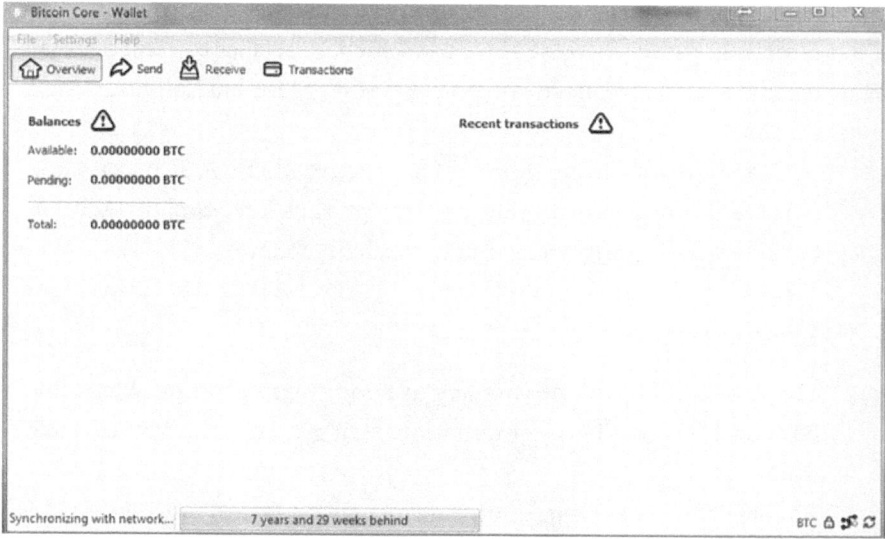

*A Full Node Bitcoin wallet*

## SPV (Simplified Payment Verification) Wallets

Unlike the full node wallet, this wallet does not keep a copy of the blockchain on your computer. It is a wallet developed basically for ease of payment. The transfer verification of such wallets are performed by full node wallets.

## Hot Wallets

Generally speaking, these are the crypto exchange and Internet-based wallets.

## Desktop Wallets

As the name suggests, these wallets can be used from the desktop of your computer and have basic interfaces.

## Mobile Wallets

Contains the wallet solutions offered for tablets, phones and all types of mobile devices.

## Cold Storage Wallets

## Paper Wallets

It is the storing of all private keys, address information and QR codes in a printed format.

## Hardware Wallets

From a distance, these hardware wallets look like external flash drives but in reality, they contain your private keys. They operate on the same principle as needing a key to start your car's engine.

## MS Wallet (Multiple Signature-"MultiSig")

For some crypto values and instances, wallets requiring multiple signatures can be used. These wallets can only be unlocked with more than one key. For instance, 3 predefined keys can be handed to 3 different people. It may be required to have at least 2 keys for any transfer out of this wallet. Therefore, the possibility of a single person vanishing with all the value is avoided.

In company bank accounts, approvals from more than one partner is required over certain sums. Multiple Signature wallets operate with the same principle.

*A paper Bitcoin wallet*

# CHAPTER FIVE

## SMART CONTRACTS

"Imagine the ideal protocol. It would have the most trustworthy third party imaginable – a diety who is on everybody's side. All the parties would send their inputs to God. God would reliably determine the results and return the outputs. God being the ultimate in confessional discretion, no party would learn anything more about the other parties' inputs than they could learn from their own inputs and the output. Alas, in the our temporal world we deal with humans rather than deities. Yet, too often we are forced to treat people in a nearly theological manner, because our infrastructure lacks the security needed to protect ourselves."

Nick Szabo, 1997, The God Protocols

CHAPTER 5

## Smart Conracts

In 1994, Nick Szabo discovered that the digital ledgers we have mentioned are actually pretty good platforms for "smart contracts." Smart contracts can be considered as digital contracts which can self-manage/conclude. These smart contracts on the blockchain are actually computer applications which are monitored by the network of all computers in the blockchain system, whose details are determined and which are ready to act on these details under desired circumstances.

Smart contracts allow for safe trading over the blockchain without the need for having an intermediary in many cases. Think about exchanging money, buying real estate or stocks with the conditions already determined, without any mediator and without any disagreement among relevant parties. It seems a bit hard with the current conventional system, doesn't it? But the smart contracts implemented on the blockchain infrastructure, which looks suspicious from a distance, are just a handful of the countless possible use cases.

Smart contracts start with the processing of the conditions, agreed upon by the parties, into the system as a computer code. The parties may opt to remain anonymous, but the monitoring and recording of the process is most certainly transparent for the computers inside the network. When the conditions, which are mutually agreed upon and included in the smart contract, are fulfilled, the

## AYN RAND WAS WRONG. ATLAS NEVER SHRUGGED: BITCOIN

contract starts and finalizes the process automatically on its own.

Let's give a more conventional example so that you can visualize the topics smart contracts:

Vending machines that accept coins can be considered as the most primitive example of smart contracts.6 For instance, you see a soda machine and you want to buy one of the products inside the machine. The smart contract in this case is as follows: if you put the correct amount of coins inside, the machine will enable you to enter the code of the soda you want. And if you enter the code for one of the products which match the amount of money you put in, the vending machine will give you that product. If you enter the wrong code, you cannot get the product, you are refunded and the contract is not fulfilled.

## 5 characteristics of smart contracts

1. They are economical; because the amount that you would normally pay as a commission or mediator's fee remains in your pocket.

2. They are autonomous; once the smart contract is coded, it will not work unless the determined conditions are met, but the contract will be be immediately enforced under the correct circumstances.

3. They are safe; you can partake in a smart contract anonymously and your information is stored in the computers of the network after being encrypted.

4. They are redundant; all transfers and transactions realized on the smart contract are backed up.

5. They are accurate; they not only prevent mistakes due to human error, but also actualize and finalize the process quite fast.

Right now, Ethereum is the biggest and most common platform used for smart contracts.

Ethereum Platform defined themselves as follows:

"Ethereum is a decentralized platform that runs smart contracts: applications that run exactly as programmed without any possibility of downtime, censorship, fraud or third-party interference.

These apps run on a custom built blockchain, an enormously powerful shared global infrastructure that can move value around and represent the ownership of property.

This enables developers to create markets, store registries of debts or promises, move funds in accordance with instructions given long in the past (like a will or a futures contract) and many other things that have not been invented yet, all without a middleman or counterparty risk.

The project was bootstrapped via an ether presale in August 2014 by fans all around the world. It is developed by the Ethereum Foundation, a Swiss non-profit, with contributions from great minds across the globe."

www.ethereum.org

If you are curious about other up-to-date and popular blockchain/open ledger systems; you can look into other systems such as Hyperledger, Openchain, Multichain, Stellar, Quorum and Hydrachain.

# CHAPTER SIX

## AREAS OF USE FOR BLOCKCHAIN TECHNOLOGY

"You can avoid the reality, but you cannot avoid the
consequences of avoiding reality"
Ayn Rand

CHAPTER SIX

# Areas of use for blockchain technology

As we mentioned in the introduction chapter, Bitcoin is just one of the opportunities provided by the blockchain technology. We can summarize the purpose of this technology as "eliminating the need for intermediaries and trusted 3rd parties." Therefore, the blockchain will revolutionize almost all industries in the future. So where can we come across blockchain apart from Bitcoin?

Blockchain is applicable to many sectors run by the existing conventional systems and actually is applied to some of them. There are hundreds of projects that are or about to be realized and their number increases day by day. Looking at various industries we may see it in; marketing, commerce, video games, insurance, mobile communications/services, finance, banking, notary services, Internet of Things, payments, crowdfunding, artificial intelligence, charity/donations, cyber-security, cloud storage services, streaming, supply chain management, healthcare, media, advertising, social networks, government services, real estate, online music services, energy management, inheritance management and so on. We are at the very beginning of duly using this technology. Imagine what might happen when we do use blockchain to its full potential...

To hammer it home, let's have a brief look in the scenarios that are already realized or about to be so in certain sectors.

## Charity Organizations/Donations

Many of us had the same suspicions in this regard: "Is my contribution really reaching to those in need??" Thanks to the blockchain technology, you can monitor whether it does or not. Because blockchain is a system where all donors can examine the whole process and the records thereof in a transparent manner. There are already certain examples at work.

## Online Music

Think about the artists and musicians whose music you enjoy. How about a platform where the licensing and publishing rights are taken care of automatically and you can pay directly to the artist? No intermediaries, no cuts. Directly from the creator to the consumer. Isn't it a less costly and more democratic model? A blockchain system built for this purpose and equipped with smart contracts can make it happen.

## Banking

With blockchain, it is possible for financial services to reach the unbanked, for reducing transaction times to mere hours or even minutes as opposed to the longer times in traditional banking, for

speeding up the verification processes, for cutting down transaction fees and for increasing efficiency while reducing energy consumption. There are already such systems in operations and the number companies jumping on the bandwagon increases each and every day.

## Elections

Reliability of elections is always in the agenda in many countries. Right or wrong, biased or unbiased, comments are abundant. "Were the votes tallied correctly?", "There is certainly a mistake!", "I doubt the transparency of this process!" Thanks to blockchain, registration, identity verification and electronic tallying of the votes can be transformed into a process that is shielded against external intervention and that can be transparently monitored by the public. Companies have begun working on this topic.

## Real Estate Services

Certainly some of us have encountered problems while buying, selling or renting real estate with regards to paperwork, transparency and missing/incorrect records. The use of blockchain can speed up all the processes involved from one and to the other, as well as providing a single platform where the process can be monitored, the property or asset records can be checked and the obtained information can be verified. Some blockchain companies have projects focusing on this sector.

## IoT (Internet of Things)

Blockchain can enable online and smart devices to work in tandem in certain areas without requiring a physical center, in a manner that is transparent and observable. There are existing and planned projects in Europe and Asia. Imagine that your vehicle, which is connected to the Internet, can pay for the fuel you buy. Or that the household appliances buy their own electricity...

## Energy Management

Energy management has been a centralized process for so long. Those that produce the energy and those who consume it cannot trade without a mediator for the most part. However, some existing and planned project allow for buying/selling transactions between the producer and the consumer through blockchain, with an ethereum-based payment. "Buying electricity without an intermediary body?" Sounds impossible, right? But it is possible with blockchain.

## Crowdfunding

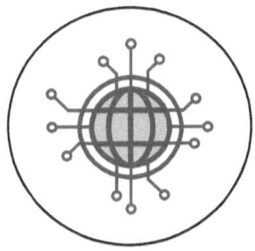

Crowdfunding has become a popular financing form lately. You can think of it as an investment method between the company trying the raise funds and the supporters who want to back their project. However, it can be quite "expensive" to participate in this system nowadays. If this method is based on the blockchain, you can buy products/services safely in return for the company's own digital currency without any mediators and with the security provided by smart contracts. Even though the regulation process still needs to be reviewed, when the system is built and operated properly, it is promising.

## Consulting

People in the consulting industry face the common questions of "Can you take a look?", "Is it possible to glance over it?," "I got what I need but can I pay you later?" There have been times where you were not able to price your own knowledge accumulated over time, you unique approach and experience. What if you provided consulting with a video call over a blockchain-integrated application and instantly received the price you set from the person/company you were consulting for?

## Video Streaming

There are a few shows that we really love watching, but we cannot purchase packages for only those shows.

We have to pay for shows that we do not like in order to watch the ones that we do like. Why? I'm not watching, but I'm still paying. What if there was a platform integrated with the blockchain infrastructure where you would directly pay for the shows you watched and didn't have to pay for those you don't?

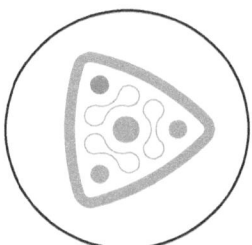

## Artworks

The world is filled with brilliant artworks. Paintings, sculptures, memorabilia, works that have witnessed important events in history...You are an art enthusiast, you follow auctions but even though you have the financial means, you may not be able to own an artwork or a piece of if the stars are not aligned. Paperwork, transportation and other process-specific procedures...So, what if these artworks were in a transparent safe where everyone could see them and were sold in shares? "Owning half of painting A by artist B" is indescribably satisfying for a passionate art aficionado, and an essential investment opportunity for an investor who has a vision. Thanks to the blockchain technology, each product/service can be divided into pieces as small as desired, and the process can be monitored by everyone.

There are many more examples and industries. But as you can see, plenty of structures and operation systems, which we always considered to be impossible, are actually possible via blockchain.

# CHAPTER SEVEN

## ICOs
## (Initial Coin Offerings)

"If Mark Zuckerberg had told me his idea,
i would have invested in it."
Anonymous

CHAPTER 7

# ICOs
# (Initial Coin Offerings)

ICOs are a whole new ball game that is neglected while talking so much about Bitcoin. Initial Coin Offering become popular with blockchain technology as an alternative to crowdfunding. To take it further, it is a system that can be an alternative to the good old stocks, shares and other traditional investment concepts.

Friedrich Hayek's dream of companies having their private currencies was not quite like this. We can say that the blockchain technology surpassed Hayek's dreams. Hayek's private currency system was a theory that didn't have a center in the beginning but could veer towards centralization in the long run.

Thanks to blockchain, which reduces the probability of the power accumulating at a single place as much as possible, a completely different economic order can be established. After two or three decades, the services/products of companies working with blockchain may only be purchased via their own currencies.

Maybe you have heard of this famous anecdote: David Choe, who designed the graffiti on the office walls of Facebook in 2005, has been given a small Facebook share instead of cash. When Facebook was taken to public, Choe's shares were worth approximately 500 million dollars. This anecdote is a utopia for those living places other than US or similar countries, where the entrepreneurship and investment ecosystems are developed...

Because there are geographical barriers...

Because there are bureaucratic barriers...

This may very well be the most exciting aspect of Bitcoin, or more precisely, the blockchain technology. Regardless of where you live; US, Russia, China or on the other end of the globe, you will be able to invest in an idea that you believe has a bright future in its infancy. Actually, you are able to do it now.

When entrepreneurs want to actualize an idea, naturally they need funding. If they have the capital, they move forward on their own. If not, they need an investor/partner that can finance their idea/company. This can be an acquaintance. But as the need for a greater capital arises, they need to find a bigger investor.

Ideas that need funding can turn to "angel investors" at the founding stages of the company. They sell a portion of the company to the investor in return for their investment. Because even if the entrepreneur has an idea, they need a certain sum to develop the first product/service and to keep the company alive until that point. But finding angel investors is not as easy as it was. The paperwork is a quite different challenge.

Idea-wise, angel investing is a very correct system. If you are not an entrepreneur or you do not have the energy to build and grow a business, you can invest in an initiative what you is promising. Yet, regardless of how good it is, this system cannot go down to the public and cannot become democratized. When a company is taken to public, it has already grown to a certain degree.

Those who gain the most by investing in a company are the people or institutions which already have large capitals. In order to become an angel investor, you need a considerable fund. Even though we think that "the Internet has eliminated boundaries", geography is still a barrier.

For instance; do you believe that an ordinary person in Germany with a modest capital could become an angel investor for Facebook as much as their capital allowed? Of course they couldn't. Let's have a brief look at the reasons;

1. First of all they wouldn't, or couldn't, even be aware that such a company was in the starting phases.
2. A small investment taken from their savings would not be enough for becoming an angel investor for Facebook.
3. There are numerous bureaucratic issues against them becoming an official partner of Facebook since they are not US citizens.

These are the obstacles that prevent smaller investors from making bigger profits and that fend angel investing away from democratization. The entrepreneurs face hurdles too.

1. It is not easy to reach out to angel investors.
2. Also, as the angel investor holds the financial power, the entrepreneur with big dreams cannot act that freely in managing the company.

## What is the difference between an ICO and an IPO?

The most common misconception about ICOs is that they are the same as IPOs. With IPOs, you own the shares of the company you invested in, so you become a partner. With ICOs, you do not buy shares of the company with your investment, so you cannot stake a claim on the company. ICOs allow you to have tokens which the company will use when selling their products/services.

Even though there are certain companies that run initial coin offerings and initial public offerings simultaneously, these are rare cases.

For instance, if Facebook was a new company and received their initial funding through an ICO, they would issue Facebook coins. These Facebook coins would be used for the services in the Facebook ecosystem (buying ads, in-game purchases, etc.). The value of the coin would be shaped according to the demand for Facebook's services.

# CHAPTER EIGHT

## WHO IS SATOSHI NAKAMOTO?

"Who is John Galt?"
Ayn Rand

CHAPTER EIGHT

## Who is Satoshi Nakamoto?

People can't comprehend "why a person who invented something that can change the world would hide himself or why he wouldn't want to take credit for such an invention." Or rather, regular people can't comprehend it. You cannot jump to conclusions without knowing the philosophical foundation of Bitcoin's idea.

You can motivate Edison with money. He can advocate something wrong to make more money, even though he knows it's wrong. But you cannot use money to motivate Tesla. You cannot dissuade him from what he believes in. You cannot use money or spare his life to dissuade Galileo from what he believes to be true. He would still claim that the Earth is round at the risk of his life.

Why did we have such an introduction? Because almost everyone looking for the answer to the "Who is Satoshi Nakamoto?" question is thinking like Edison. And this reasoning leads to faulty results. As a matter of fact, the general result is an exaggerated one, such as "The United States, the powers that be, etc..."

### Who is John Galt?

In the novel Atlas Shrugged authored by Ayn Rand, the moral defender of capitalism, all the people who work, contribute and produce start disappearing one by one. These people are kidnapped by someone with the pseudonym of John Galt. And the whole country is asking the question, "Who is John Galt?"

# AYN RAND WAS WRONG. ATLAS NEVER SHRUGGED: BITCOIN

John Galt is also the inventor of "a Utopian engine running on static electricity", which no one can understand or operate. But he stopped working on the engine and disappeared. John Galt's disappearance and his kidnapping of productive and creative people symbolizes that Atlas, the Greek God who carries the world on his back, would no longer do so. Atlas shrugged.

By the end of the book, we understand that John Galt took these people to a secret valley, a utopian paradise. In this paradise, gold is used as currency, not the dollar. The reason can be understood from the following section.

"Whenever destroyers appear among men, they start by destroying money, for money is men's protection and the base of a moral existence. Destroyers seize gold and leave to its owners a counterfeit pile of paper. This kills all objective standards and delivers men into the arbitrary power of an arbitrary setter of values. Gold was an objective value, an equivalent of wealth produced. Paper is a mortgage on wealth that does not exist, backed by a gun aimed at those who are expected to produce it. Paper is a check drawn by legal looters upon an account which is not theirs: upon the virtue of the victims. Watch for the day when it becomes, marked: 'Account overdrawn.'"

Bitcoin is a brand new alternative to the gold standard ceased to exist. It is humanity's way of rediscovering the physical standards that were lost after gold was virtualized with dozens of derivatives as well. It is even more tangible than gold. The supply of gold in nature is limited, but we do not know what this limit is. A brand new gold reserve may be found somewhere on the world tomorrow.

> *"US Federal Reserve (FED) does not have the authority to regulate the cryptocurrency."*
>
> *Janet Yellen, US FED Chair, February 27, 2014*

However, Bitcoin is mathematically limited. No Bitcoin reserve will be found anywhere at any time. It is not connected to any state. It is not under the control of any government or authority. No state can mint new Bitcoins or decrease its supply arbitrarily. There is no central bank behind Bitcoin. On the contrary, Bitcoin is an alternative to all the central banks in the world. It is not dependent on humane elements such as arbitrariness or personal desire. It is directly based on mathematical rules, the law of the universe.

That's why the pseudonym Satoshi Nakamoto represents John Galt, or Atlas, who carries the world on his shoulders. His identity is a mystery, just like John Galt's. But unlike Galt, he didn't give up.

## So why is Satoshi Nakamoto still a mystery?

1) We mentioned that humanity used the bounty of the nature as money since day one. It means that, humans trusted a free currency that wasn't tied to anyone. People who chased the idea of Bitcoin for years against the increasingly virtualized currencies that were subjugated by states, were pure capitalists. In order for the revolution to succeed, Bitcoin needed to be transformed into an asset that was gifted to humanity by nature. For this reason, it was crucial that the inventor(s) remained a mystery. Because you cannot separate any invention from its inventor. For example, no cryptocurrency other than Bitcoin can be evaluated independently of its inventor. A mistake, a good deer or opinion of the inventor has a direct effect on the value of said cryptocurrency. This leads people

> *"Bitcoin is better than gold and the U.S. dollar. Bitcoin is mathematically defined, there is a certain quantity of bitcoin, there's a way it's distributed... and it's pure and there's no human running, there's no company running and it's just... growing and growing... and surviving, that to me says something that is natural and nature is more important than all our human conventions"*
>
> Steve Wozniak, Founding Partner of Apple

to have a sentiment like it's a stock, not a currency.

With its inventor a mystery, Bitcoin turned into something that everyone could adopt and have an opinion on. Just like gold, silver, pearls and sea shells, it is both a gift of nature and it is limited in supply.

2) There are two kinds of inventions. For example, if Newton did not discover gravity, gravity would still continue to exist. Or, without Archimedes, buoyancy of water would still cause objects to float or sink. But there are certain inventions that erase the past and rewrite the future.

If you have read the book so far, you probably understand that the idea of Bitcoin is not just about Bitcoin itself. Bitcoin and, by extension, the blockchain technology is going to revolutionize all modes of trading, human relations and law in the world. To take it a step further, it will transform the concept of state and its role in human lives, as we have covered in the prologue. The creator of such a disruptive technology probably wouldn't lead a very comfortable life. Considering the fact that Phil Zimmerman, the inventor of PGP (Pretty Good Privacy - an encrypted electronic mail system) was questioned for 3 years, what would happen to Satoshi Nakamoto? Also, given that Bernard von Nothaus, the founder of the Liberty Dollar "private currency system", which is based on precious metals such as gold and silver, was arrested in 2009, we can say that the

*Adam Back, inventor of Hashcash*

reasons for Nakamoto's anonymity are quite well-founded.

The inventor(s) of Bitcoin never revealed their identities or went public for these reasons and probably many more that we don't know of. Moreover, after creating the system, they gave up around 1,200,000 Bitcoins they generated while creating the first blocks required for the security of the system. (As of April 2018, this is a fortune worth approximately 15-20 billion dollars, including the other cryptocurrencies they earner from the Bitcoin forks.) Around 1,200,000 Bitcoins are still staying put in those wallets.

## What does Satoshi Nakamoto mean?

There is likely an allusion in the pseudonym chosen by the creator of Bitcoin; because it is a manifest by nature, it is attempting to create an alternative future and it already contains a jab at the deviance of the existing financial system in its Genesis block.

Looking at the match-ups of the Japanese words Satoshi and Nakamoto, the meaning that is closest to the spirit of Bitcoin is this:

"Phoenix rising from the ashes of centralization"

## Who may be Satoshi Nakamoto?

Who gave up on a fortune worth 15-20 billion dollars as of April 2018? Who turned away from a possible Nobel Prize in economy? Who chose to be included in the Forbes richest people list with a "nickname?" Who didn't take the credit for a world-changing invention? Who had an ego so high that he didn't need other people to applaud him? Who chose to go down in history with a pseudonym? There have been countless arguments about who this person or these people he might be.

There are three people who supported the idea of a stateless currency, who built their own systems and who never gave up on the idea.

## 1) Nick Szabo

Considering that Bitcoin is at the crossroads of law, economy and technology, the most likely candidate for Satoshi Nakamoto is Nick Szabo, if Nakamoto is not a group of people.

Creator of the smart contract concept, Szabo states that realizing the fact that contracts can be created digitally in an encrypted manner, he decided to study law and graduated in 2006. Having worked at David Chaum's DigiCash for a year, Nick Szabo has all the knowledge necessary for creating Bitcoin.

Thinking about the ideal structure of Bitcoin, which shakes the concept of currency to the core, we can argue that Szabo's article titled "Origins of Money" lays the economic foundation of Bitcoin. Likewise, Szabo says that he got the same "money is not such a thing" answer from every economist he defined money to. According to classical economists money is a tool for "value transfer," whereas Nick Szabo is primarily a tool for "wealth accumulation" and "inheritance for coming generations."

Szabo invented BitGold, the progenitor of Bitcoin, in 1998 and shared this idea in a closed mail group. In April 2008, Szabo published his BitGold idea in his public blog. In the comment section, he states that he figured out the answers to the questions in his mind regarding Bitgold and that he was looking for someone to help him with the software. But this blog entry was removed after the Bitcoin article was published and it was re-posted after changing the date.

Furthermore, following the 2008 crisis, Szabo wrote in his blog that the existing financial system has collapsed and the new financial system was needed.

We wouldn't be exaggerating when we say that Szabo is the most obsessed person when it comes to "trusted 3rd parties," considering his statement about the only 3rd party that would be acceptable in transactions between two people could be "God" in his suitable titled "God Protocols" article.

Saying that there are three people, including himself, that never gave up on the idea of a currency not tied to any state, Nick Szabo's long silence after the Bitcoin article is published seems to support the argument that he is Satoshi Nakamoto.

When you read about the ideas that came before Bitcoin, you may think about "why Bitcoin was this late" or "everything necessary for Bitcoin had already been found." There have been many people who thought like this and said it out loud. The fact that Szabo, who remained silent for so long about Bitcoin, wrote his second article on Bitcoin with the title "Why Did It Took So Long to Create Bitcoin?" in 2011 and that he tells why Bitcoin is not that of an obvious idea make things even more interesting.

If you take a look at Szabo's blog, the first thing you will notice that all of his writing follows an almost academic format. But there is one blog post that is an exception. Szabo shared a funny video on January 31, 2009, and it can be seen that this video alludes to the "double spending" problem solved by Bitcoin.7

And then there is this blunder by Nick Szabo during his interview with Tim Ferriss. He blurts out: "when I designed Bitcoin...", and immediately corrects himself by saying "BitGold", thus cementing the claims that Szabo is indeed Satoshi Nakamoto.

## 2) Hal Finney

Being a Cypherpunk, the second engineer of PGP after Phil Zimmermann and the creator of RPOW shows that Hal Finney has the capability and the philosophical background for creating Bitcoin.

## WHO IS SATOSHI NAKAMOTO?

When Nakamoto shared the first Bitcoin article in the cryptography mail group, everyone was skeptical and believed it to be impossible, whereas Hal Finney was the first to support Nakamoto.

People laid out their doubts in the first e-mails, while Hal Finney was responding to these doubts. Hal Finney started working on Bitcoin together with Satoshi Nakamoto. They communicated solely via e-mail. Bitcoin operating like the RPOW developed by Hal Finney strengthened the argument that Finney was Nakamoto.

On top of that, he was the first person Nakamoto transferred money for testing.

Another interesting thing is that, Dorian Satoshi Nakamoto, who appeared on media, was living only two blocks away from Hal Finney's house.

Spending his last years as an ALS patient, Finney always rejected such claims. Finney passed away in 2014 and had his body cryogenically frozen by Alcor Life Extension Foundation until the day humanity achieves immortality. It is claimed that Finney spent a portion his Bitcoins for the treatment of his disease and this cryogenic procedure.

Never having spent more than 1 million Bitcoins, maybe Nakamoto is someone who believes immortality can be achieved, who knows?

*Hal Finney's tweet from January 10, 2009; stating that he is running the Bitcoin software. Bitcoin software was first run by Satoshi Nakamoto on January 3, 2009.*

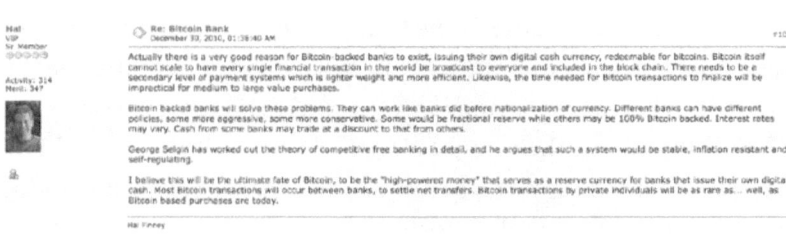

## 3) Wei Dai

Satoshi Nakamoto stated that Bitcoin is the realized version of Nick Szabo's BitGold and Wei Dai's b-money. Wei Dai is also the second person contacted by Nakamoto before he published the Bitcoin article to make a reference. After Bitcoin made headlines and the speculations about its creator increased, Dai shared his communications with Nakamoto via the press. Maybe that's why the possibility of him being Nakamoto was not considered too much.

But, due to the fact that he is a cypherpunk, he developed b-money in 1997 and he cares about his personal privacy; the possibility of Dai being Nakamoto should not be ruled out.

## 4) National Security Agency of the United States / The powers that be, etc...

For those who fail to analyze the world for a period longer than their lives or 50-100 years and those that do not believe that "a different world is possible," the answer to Satoshi Nakamoto's identity is pretty easy: National Security Agency of the United States, the powers that be, etc...

The fact that more than 1 million Bitcoins remain unspent and Satoshi Nakamoto is still a mystery is the biggest argument for the-

> Just as the smallest unit of Bitcoin is called Satoshi after its creator; smaller units of Ethereum are named after Szabo, Finney and Wei.

se people.

The most marketable and convincing argument of the defenders of such claims is the cover of the Economist from January 1988. It is natural that ordinary people come to this conclusion after seeing the cover; but the fact that all those professors make such assertions by looking at this cover is just sad.

The cover of the Economist from January 1988 shows a gold-like coin on a chain around the neck of a phoenix rising from the ashes of burning dollars. The date on the coin is 2018. The tagline on the cover is: "Get ready for a world currency"

Makes so much sense, right? No, it does not. Because no one, including those great professors, bothers to read the cover story inside the magazine.

The story advocates that a single global currency would be better for "monetary policies" and "inflation." It says that a mismanaged monetary policy in one country would hurt not only her own economy, but also the economy of others in a world without walls or borders.

# AYN RAND WAS WRONG. ATLAS NEVER SHRUGGED: BITCOIN

# CHAPTER NINE

## BITCOIN WHITE PAPER

"Internet is going to be one of the major forces for reducing the role of government. The one thing that's missing but soon will be developed is a reliable e-cash"

Milton Friedman

## CHAPTER NINE

## Bitcoin Whitepaper

You have seen Bitcoin on newspapers, magazines, TV and the Internet. You started hearing about it quite frequently while chatting with your friends. You read the stories about those who became rich thanks to Bitcoin and started wondering; "what is Bitcoin?" You asked your friends who were interested in it; you searched it on the web. On top of all that, you bought and read this book. Instead of reading the article where Satoshi Nakamoto, the inventor of Bitcion, proposes a new financial system, you conducted your research from dozens of other sources. Now, let's hear what Bitcoin is and how it works from its creator.

# Bitcoin:
# A Peer-to-Peer Elektronic Cash System

Satoshi Nakamoto
satoshin@gmx.com
www.bitcoin.org

**Abstract:**
A purely peer-to-peer version of electronic cash would allow online payments to be sent directly from one party to another without going through a financial institution. Digital signatures provide part of the solution, but the main benefits are lost if a trusted third party is still required to prevent double-spending. We propose a solution to the double-spending problem using a peer-to-peer network. The network timestamps transactions by hashing them into an ongoing chain of hash-based proof-of-work, forming a record that cannot be changed without redoing the proof-of-work. The longest chain not only serves as proof of the sequence of events witnessed, but proof that it came from the largest pool of CPU power. As long as a majority of CPU power is controlled by nodes that are not cooperating to attack the network, they will generate the longest chain and outpace attackers. The network itself requires minimal structure. Messages are broadcast on a best effort basis, and nodes can leave and rejoin the network at will, accepting the longest proof-of-work chain as proof of what happened while they were gone.

## 1) Introduction

Commerce on the Internet has come to rely almost exclusively on financial institutions serving as trusted third parties to process electronic payments. While the system works well enough for most transactions, it still suffers from the inherent weaknesses of the trust based model. Completely non-reversible transactions are not really possible, since financial institutions cannot avoid mediating disputes. The cost of mediation increases transaction costs, limiting the minimum practical transaction size and cutting off the possibility for small casual transactions, and there is a broader cost in the loss of ability to make non-reversible payments for non-reversible services. With the possibility of reversal, the need for trust spreads. Merchants must be wary of their customers, hassling them for more information than they would otherwise need. A certain percentage of fraud is accepted as unavoidable. These costs and payment uncertainties can be avoided in person by using physical currency, but no mechanism exists to make payments over a communications channel without a trusted party.

What is needed is an electronic payment system based on cryptographic proof instead of trust, allowing any two willing parties to transact directly with each other without the need for a trusted third party. Transactions that are computationally impractical to reverse would protect sellers from fraud, and routine escrow mechanisms could easily be implemented to protect buyers. In this paper, we propose a solution to the double-spending problem using a peer-to-peer distributed timestamp server to generate computational proof of the chronological order of transactions. The system is secure as long as honest nodes collectively control more CPU power than any cooperating group of attacker nodes.

## 2) Transactions

We define an electronic coin as a chain of digital signatures. Each owner transfers the coin to the next by digitally signing a hash of the previous transaction and the public key of the next owner and adding these to the end of the coin. A payee can verify the signatures to verify the chain of ownership.

The problem of course is the payee can't verify that one of the owners did not double-spend the coin. A common solution is to introduce a trusted central authority, or mint, that checks every transaction for double spending. After each transaction, the coin must be returned to the mint to issue a new coin, and only coins issued directly from the mint are trusted not to be double-spent. The problem with this solution is that the fate of the entire money system depends on the company running the mint, with every transaction having to go through them, just like a bank.

We need a way for the payee to know that the previous owners did not sign any earlier transactions. For our purposes, the earliest transaction is the one that counts, so we don't care about later attempts to double-spend. The only way to confirm the absence

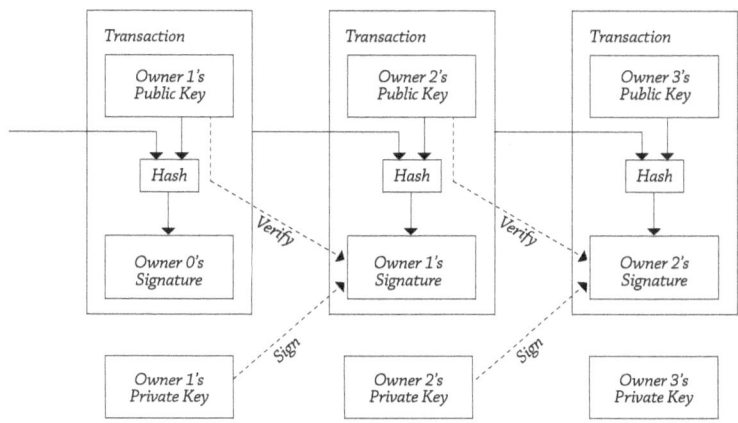

of a transaction is to be aware of all transactions. In the mint based model, the mint was aware of all transactions and decided which arrived first. To accomplish this without a trusted party, transactions must be publicly announced[1], and we need a system for participants to agree on a single history of the order in which they were received. The payee needs proof that at the time of each transaction, the majority of nodes agreed it was the first received.

## 3) Timestamp Server

The solution we propose begins with a timestamp server. A timestamp server works by taking a hash of a block of items to be timestamped and widely publishing the hash, such as in a newspaper or Usenet post.[2-5] The timestamp proves that the data must have existed at the time, obviously, in order to get into the hash. Each timestamp includes the previous timestamp in its hash, forming a chain, with each additional timestamp reinforcing the ones before it.

## 4) Proof-of-Work

To implement a distributed timestamp server on a peer-to-peer basis, we will need to use a proof-of-work system similar to Adam Back's Hashcash[6], rather than newspaper or Usenet posts. The proof-of-work involves scanning for a value that when hashed,

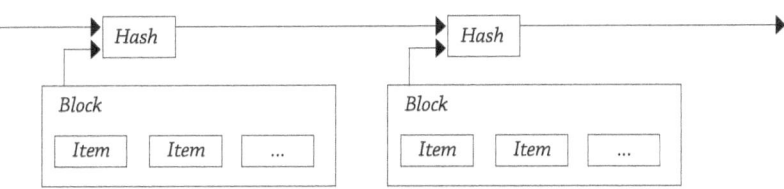

such as with SHA-256, the hash begins with a number of zero bits. The average work required is exponential in the number of zero bits required and can be verified by executing a single hash.

For our timestamp network, we implement the proof-of-work by incrementing a nonce in the block until a value is found that gives the block's hash the required zero bits. Once the CPU effort has been expended to make it satisfy the proof-of-work, the block cannot be changed without redoing the work. As later blocks are chained after it, the work to change the block would include redoing all the blocks after it.

The proof-of-work also solves the problem of determining representation in majority decision making. If the majority were based on one-IP-address-one-vote, it could be subverted by anyone able to allocate many IPs. Proof-of-work is essentially one-CPU-one-vote. The majority decision is represented by the longest chain, which has the greatest proof-of-work effort invested in it. If a majority of CPU power is controlled by honest nodes, the honest

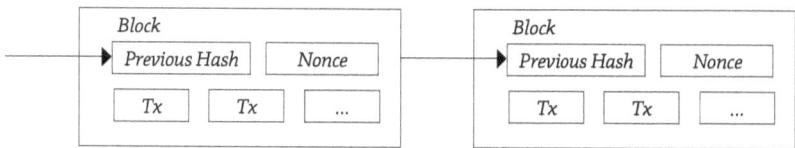

chain will grow the fastest and outpace any competing chains. To modify a past block, an attacker would have to redo the proof-of-work of the block and all blocks after it and then catch up with and surpass the work of the honest nodes. We will show later that the probability of a slower attacker catching up diminishes exponentially as subsequent blocks are added.

To compensate for increasing hardware speed and varying interest in running nodes over time, the proof-of-work difficulty is determined by a moving average targeting an average number of blocks per hour. If they're generated too fast, the difficulty increases.

## 5) Network

The steps to run the network are as follows:
New transactions are broadcast to all nodes.
Each node collects new transactions into a block.
Each node works on finding a difficult proof-of-work for its block.
When a node finds a proof-of-work, it broadcasts the block to all nodes.
Nodes accept the block only if all transactions in it are valid and not already spent.
Nodes express their acceptance of the block by working on creating the next block in the chain, using the hash of the accepted block as the previous hash.

Nodes always consider the longest chain to be the correct one and will keep working on extending it. If two nodes broadcast different versions of the next block simultaneously, some nodes may receive one or the other first. In that case, they work on the first one they received, but save the other branch in case it becomes longer. The tie will be broken when the next proof-of-work is found and one branch becomes longer; the nodes that were working on the other branch will then switch to the longer one.

New transaction broadcasts do not necessarily need to reach all nodes. As long as they reach many nodes, they will get into a block before long. Block broadcasts are also tolerant of dropped messages. If a node does not receive a block, it will request it when it receives the next block and realizes it missed one.

## 6) Incentive

By convention, the first transaction in a block is a special transaction that starts a new coin owned by the creator of the block. This adds an incentive for nodes to support the network, and provides a way to initially distribute coins into circulation, since there is no central authority to issue them. The steady addition of a constant of amount of new coins is analogous to gold miners expending resources to add gold to circulation. In our case, it is CPU time and electricity that is expended.

The incentive can also be funded with transaction fees. If the output value of a transaction is less than its input value, the difference is a transaction fee that is added to the incentive value of the block containing the transaction. Once a predetermined number of coins have entered circulation, the incentive can transition entirely to transaction fees and be completely inflation free.

The incentive may help encourage nodes to stay honest. If a greedy attacker is able to assemble more CPU power than all the honest nodes, he would have to choose between using it to defraud people by stealing back his payments, or using it to generate new coins. He ought to find it more profitable to play by the rules, such rules that favour him with more new coins than everyone else combined, than to undermine the system and the validity of his own wealth.

## 7) Reclaiming Disk Space

Once the latest transaction in a coin is buried under enough blocks, the spent transactions before it can be discarded to save disk space.

To facilitate this without breaking the block's hash, transactions are hashed in a Merkle Tree[7-2-5], with only the root included in the block's hash. Old blocks can then be compacted by stubbing off branches of the tree. The interior hashes do not need to be stored.

A block header with no transactions would be about 80 bytes. If we suppose blocks are generated every 10 minutes, 80 bytes * 6 * 24 * 365 = 4.2MB per year. With computer systems typically selling with 2GB of RAM as of 2008, and Moore's Law predicting current growth of 1.2GB per year, storage should not be a problem even if the block headers must be kept in memory.

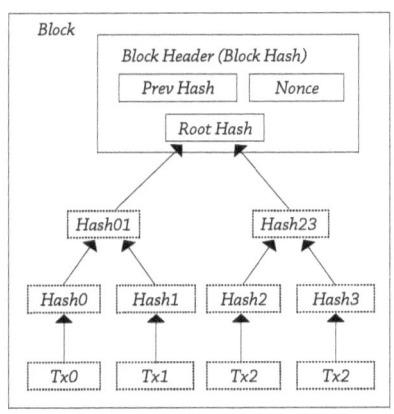

Transactions Hashed in a Merkle Tree

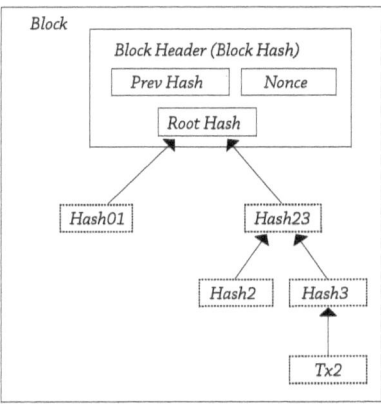

After Pruning Tx0-2 from the Block

## 8) Simplified Payment Verification

It is possible to verify payments without running a full network node. A user only needs to keep a copy of the block headers of the longest proof-of-work chain, which he can get by querying network nodes until he's convinced he has the longest chain, and obtain the Merkle branch linking the transaction to the block it's timestamped in. He can't check the transaction for himself, but by linking it to a place in the chain, he can see that a network node has accepted it, and blocks added after it further confirm the network has accepted it.

As such, the verification is reliable as long as honest nodes control the network, but is more vulnerable if the network is overpowered by an attacker. While network nodes can verify transactions for themselves, the simplified method can be fooled by an attacker's fabricated transactions for as long as the attacker can continue to overpower the network. One strategy to protect against this would be to accept alerts from network nodes when they detect an invalid block, prompting the user's software to download the full block and alerted transactions to confirm the inconsistency. Businesses that receive frequent payments will probably still want to run their own nodes for more independent security and quicker verification.

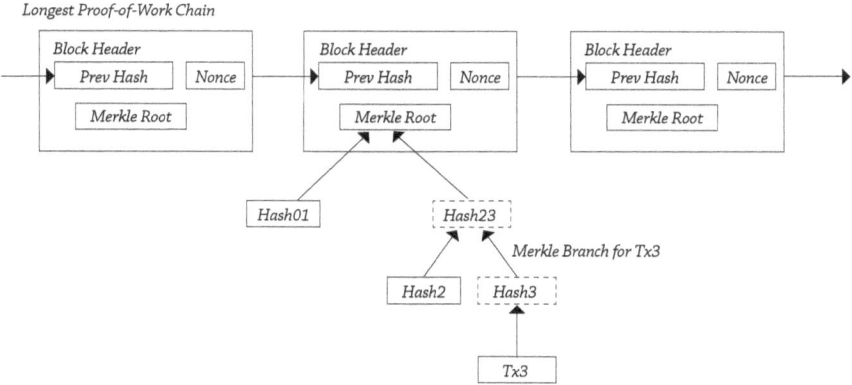

## 9) Combining and Splitting Value

Although it would be possible to handle coins individually, it would be unwieldy to make a separate transaction for every cent in a transfer. To allow value to be split and combined, transactions contain multiple inputs and outputs. Normally there will be either a single input from a larger previous transaction or multiple inputs combining smaller amounts, and at most two outputs: one for the payment, and one returning the change, if any, back to the sender.

It should be noted that fan-out, where a transaction depends on several transactions, and those transactions depend on many more, is not a problem here. There is never the need to extract a complete standalone copy of a transaction's history.

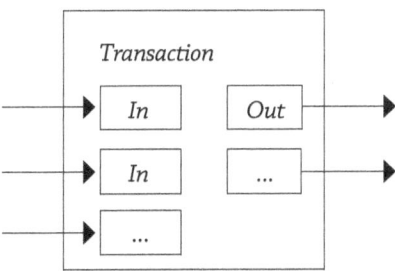

## 10) Privacy

The traditional banking model achieves a level of privacy by limiting access to information to the parties involved and the trusted third party. The necessity to announce all transactions publicly precludes this method, but privacy can still be maintained by breaking the flow of information in another place: by keeping public keys anonymous. The public can see that someone is sending an amount to someone else, but without information linking the transaction to anyone. This is similar to the level of information released by

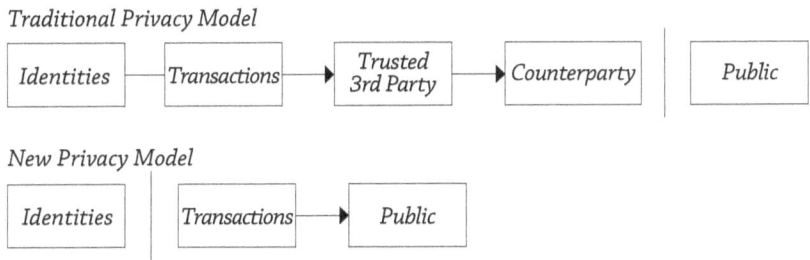

stock exchanges, where the time and size of individual trades, the "tape", is made public, but without telling who the parties were.

As an additional firewall, a new key pair should be used for each transaction to keep them from being linked to a common owner. Some linking is still unavoidable with multi-input transactions, which necessarily reveal that their inputs were owned by the same owner. The risk is that if the owner of a key is revealed, linking could reveal other transactions that belonged to the same owner.

## 11) Calculations

We consider the scenario of an attacker trying to generate an alternate chain faster than the honest chain. Even if this is accomplished, it does not throw the system open to arbitrary changes, such as creating value out of thin air or taking money that never belonged to the attacker. Nodes are not going to accept an invalid transaction as payment, and honest nodes will never accept a block containing them. An attacker can only try to change one of his own transactions to take back money he recently spent.

The race between the honest chain and an attacker chain can be characterized as a Binomial Random Walk. The success event is the honest chain being extended by one block, increasing its lead by +1, and the failure event is the attacker's chain being extended by one block, reducing the gap by -1.

The probability of an attacker catching up from a given deficit is analogous to a Gambler's Ruin problem. Suppose a gambler with unlimited credit starts at a deficit and plays potentially an infinite number of trials to try to reach breakeven. We can calculate the probability he ever reaches breakeven, or that an attacker ever catches up with the honest chain, as follows[8]:

p = probability an honest node finds the next block

q = probability the attacker finds the next block

$q_z$ = probability the attacker will ever catch up from z blocks behind

$$q_z = \begin{cases} 1 & \text{if } p \leq q \\ (q/p)^z & \text{if } p > q \end{cases}$$

Given our assumption that p>q, the probability drops exponentially as the number of blocks the attacker has to catch up with increases. With the odds against him, if he doesn't make a lucky lunge forward early on, his chances become vanishingly small as he falls further behind.

We now consider how long the recipient of a new transaction needs to wait before being sufficiently certain the sender can't change the transaction. We assume the sender is an attacker who wants to make the recipient believe he paid him for a while, then switch it to pay back to himself after some time has passed. The receiver will be alerted when that happens, but the sender hopes it will be too late.

The receiver generates a new key pair and gives the public key to the sender shortly before signing. This prevents the sender from preparing a chain of blocks ahead of time by working on it continuously until he is lucky enough to get far enough ahead, then executing the transaction at that moment. Once the transaction is sent, the dishonest sender starts working in secret on a parallel chain containing an alternate version of his transaction.

The recipient waits until the transaction has been added to a block and z blocks have been linked after it. He doesn't know the exact amount of progress the attacker has made, but assuming the honest blocks took the average expected time per block, the attacker's potential progress will be a Poisson distribution with expected value:

$$\lambda = z \frac{q}{p}$$

To get the probability the attacker could still catch up now, we multiply the Poisson density for each amount of progress he could have made by the probability he could catch up from that point:

$$\sum_{k=0}^{\infty} \frac{\lambda^k e^{-\lambda}}{k!} \cdot \begin{cases} (q/p)^{(z-k)} & \text{if } k \leq z \\ 1 & \text{if } k > z \end{cases}$$

Rearranging to avoid summing the infinite tail of the distribution...

$$1 - \sum_{k=>}^{z} \frac{\lambda^k e^{-\lambda}}{k!} \left(1 - (q/p)^{(z-k)}\right)$$

**Converting to C code...**

```
#include <math.h>
  double AttackerSuccessProbability(double q, int z)
  {
    double p = 1.0 - q;
    double lambda = z * (q / p);
    double sum = 1.0;
    int i, k;
    for (k = 0; k <= z; k++)
    {
       double poisson = exp(-lambda);
       for (i = 1; i <= k; i++)
          poisson *= lambda / i;
       sum -= poisson * (1 - pow(q / p, z - k));
    }
  return sum; }
```

Running some results, we can see the probability drop off

exponentially with z.

```
q=0.1
   z=0   P=1.0000000
   z=1   P=0.2045873
   z=2   P=0.0509779
   z=3   P=0.0131722
   z=4   P=0.0034552
   z=5   P=0.0009137
   z=6   P=0.0002428
   z=7   P=0.0000647
   z=8   P=0.0000173
   z=9   P=0.0000046
   z=10  P=0.0000012
q=0.3
   z=0   P=1.0000000
   z=5   P=0.1773523
   z=10  P=0.0416605
   z=15  P=0.0101008
   z=20  P=0.0024804
   z=25  P=0.0006132
   z=30  P=0.0001522
   z=35  P=0.0000379
   z=40  P=0.0000095
   z=45  P=0.0000024
   z=50  P=0.0000006
```

Solving for P less than 0.1%...

```
P < 0.001
   q=0.10  z=5
   q=0.15  z=8
   q=0.20  z=11
```

q=0.25  z=15
q=0.30  z=24
q=0.35  z=41
q=0.40  z=89
q=0.45  z=340

## 12) Conclusion

We have proposed a system for electronic transactions without relying on trust. We started with the usual framework of coins made from digital signatures, which provides strong control of ownership, but is incomplete without a way to prevent double-spending. To solve this, we proposed a peer-to-peer network using proof-of-work to record a public history of transactions that quickly becomes computationally impractical for an attacker to change if honest nodes control a majority of CPU power. The network is robust in its unstructured simplicity. Nodes work all at once with little coordination. They do not need to be identified, since messages are not routed to any particular place and only need to be delivered on a best effort basis. Nodes can leave and rejoin the network at will, accepting the proof-of-work chain as proof of what happened while they were gone. They vote with their CPU power, expressing their acceptance of valid blocks by working on extending them and rejecting invalid blocks by refusing to work on them. Any needed rules and incentives can be enforced with this consensus mechanism.

## References

[1] W. Dai, "b-money," http://www.weidai.com/bmoney.txt, 1998.

[2] H. Massias, X.S. Avila, and J.-J. Quisquater, "Design of a secure timestamping service with minimal trust requirements," In 20th Symposium on Information Theory in the Benelux, May 1999.

[3] S. Haber, W.S. Stornetta, "How to time-stamp a digital document," In Journal of Cryptology, vol 3, no
2, pages 99-111, 1991.

[4] D. Bayer, S. Haber, W.S. Stornetta, "Improving the efficiency and reliability of digital time-stamping," In Sequences II: Methods in Communication, Security and Computer Science, pages 329-334, 1993.

[5] S. Haber, W.S. Stornetta, "Secure names for bit-strings," In Proceedings of the 4th ACM Conference on Computer and Communications Security, pages 28-35, April 1997.

[6] A. Back, "Hashcash - a denial of service counter-measure," http://www.hashcash.org/papers/hashcash.pdf, 2002.

[7] R.C. Merkle, "Protocols for public key cryptosystems," In Proc. 1980 Symposium on Security and
Privacy, IEEE Computer Society, pages 122-133, April 1980.

[8] W. Feller, "An introduction to probability theory and its applications," 1957.

## AYN RAND WAS WRONG. ATLAS NEVER SHRUGGED: BITCOIN

# CHAPTER 10

## WHAT WILL BE THE VALUE OF BITCOIN?

"Many see crypto through the lens of overnight riches. What they don't realize is that the core creators would give up every cent they own in exchange for seeing a decentralized future become reality. This is why price swings and crashes are irrelevant to long term success."

Ryan Breslow

CHAPTER 10

# What Will Be the Value of Bitcoin?

1 Bitcoin = 1 Bitcoin
One in a 21 million total reserve…
Today, tomorrow, and centuries later…

## THANKS

To Çağrı Çelik, for introducing us to each other... Without him, this book would not exist. We'd like to thank Ece Çelik for encouraging us to write and editing our work; Sergen Bayram for the cover design and the Atlas illustration; Serdar Özen for the Bitcoin modeling on the cover; Özge Şatır and Türker Balkar for providing a different perspective with their comments; Tansel Kaya for the invaluable feedback after the first read-through and, of course, our families for their constant support.

# REFERENCES

1. https://www.theguardian.com/world/2010/nov/20/eric-cantona-bank-protest-campaign
2) Nick Szabo, Twitter post (@NickSzabo4), December 5, 2017.
3) http://www.wiki-zero.net/index.php?q=aHR0cHM6Ly9lbi53aWtpcGVkaWEub3JnL3dpa2kvR29sZF9kb2xsYXI
4  https://cryptome.org/jya/digicrash.htm
5) http://groups.csail.mit.edu/mac/classes/6.805/articles/export/zimmermann-oct93.txt
6) The Idea of Smart Contracts, Nick Szabo
   http://www.fon.hum.uva.nl/rob/Courses/InformationInSpeech/CDROM/Literature/LOTwinterschool2006/szabo.best.vwh.net/idea.html
7) Who I believe is Satoshi Nakamoto and Why - New Evidence
   SP Hodler, Youtube Video
   https://www.youtube.com/watch?v=QYtfZeJr3C0

\*\* *nakamotoinstitute.org* & *bitcointalk.org*

www.ingramcontent.com/pod-product-compliance
Lightning Source LLC
Chambersburg PA
CBHW030644220526
45463CB00004B/1630